How Pictures Mean

How Pictures Mean

Illustrated
with 92 Black and White Photographs

by
Hans Hess

PANTHEON BOOKS
A Division of Random House, New York

First American Edition

Copyright © 1974 by Hans Hess

All rights reserved under International and Pan-American Copyright Conventions. Published in the United States by Pantheon Books, a division of Random House, Inc., New York. Originally published in Great Britain as Pictures As Arguments. Published for Sussex University Press by Chatto & Windus Ltd.

Manufactured in the United States of America

Library of Congress Cataloging in Publication Data

Hess, Hans, art curator.
How Pictures Mean.

London ed. published under title: Pictures as Arguments.
    Includes bibliographical references and index.
    1. Painting—Themes, motives. 2. Painting—Psychological aspects. I. Title.
ND1145.H47 1975   750′.1   74-26195
ISBN 0-394-49765-1
ISBN 0-394-73057-7 pbk.

Contents

Introduction

There are many ways of understanding an event; the very way of understanding it, however, changes the event which has been understood. This is a simple form of stating that an event is one thing as it has happened and another thing as it is comprehended, and of the comprehension there are many forms.

This is a necessary statement if one wants to approach an understanding of modern art. The book itself follows this approach. It is not a complete history of any one artist or artistic movement, it is not even a systematic analysis of modern art. It is an attempt to reveal a mode of comprehending pictures in their relation to the artist and the situation in which he finds himself. There are many more things to be said about everything; this book says only some things about some things.

The point of this introduction, then, is to state clearly that this is not a textbook – the book is the text. It is about other texts which are the pictures in the book. These are not used as illustrations, they are arguments, and it is the aim of this book to help an understanding of pictures as arguments.

Wittgenstein has said that propositions are pictures of reality:[1] this book suggests that pictures may be propositions of reality.

When we think of the expression of 'ideas' we usually think of the written or spoken word, which is the accepted form of the expression of thought. Yet we know that thought is expressed by scientists not in words but in a language of symbols which becomes the current equivalent for the reality it attempts to describe. In the same way painters use a language, not of words, but of forms or symbols, to depict a form of reality. This reality is neither objective nor subjective, it is collective; the forms are pictorial equivalents for conventions of social and spiritual life. Painting is the outcome of thought and intention just as much as a book or a scientific paper. The fact that artists have to have special skills of a manual kind does not distinguish them from scientists. The quality of their skill is important, because it remains visible in their work, but their thought, which remains invisible, is nevertheless there and can be read. The case I am making has already been made by Leonardo da Vinci, who wrote in his 'Paragone' (which forms part of his *Trattato della Pittura*): 'As the Scribes have had no knowledge of the science of painting, they could not assign to it its rightful place or share; and painting does not display her accomplishment in words – therefore she was classed below the sciences, through ignorance . . .'[2] To remedy such ignorance is one purpose of this book.

1

The Pre-History of Modern Art

What is art? A definition by Paul Frankl reads: 'Art is the particular interrelationship of form and meaning, in which form becomes the symbol of meaning.'[3] What is superficially called style is the outward appearance of an intention; forms of art correspond to the intention, they are not freely shaped and wilfully varied, not even in the freest and most wilful forms of modern art. Pictorial art is a language of signs in which ideas are expressed.

Several years ago a volume appeared, edited by the late Sir Herbert Read,[4] which accompanied an exhibition entitled '40,000 Years of Modern Art'. It was a selection of articles trying to prove that modern art forms have always existed. The fault was simple and obvious: by treating pictorial art as a surface phenomenon, by looking at a picture only for what you can see on the surface, not much can be learned. A picture by Klee looks somewhat like a cave painting. But the significance of a work of art does not lie in a surface resemblance to something else, it is embedded in the meaning with which society has imbued the image. The social and spiritual function of a cave painting and a work by Paul Klee are literally worlds apart, and any failure to see the work, as the outcome of a social reality must lead to superficiality and error of interpretation.

A different view with similar consequences is represented in the writings of Malraux, who stipulates an eternal modern art. We can only comprehend works of the past in his 'imaginary museum' as works of our time and sensibility transposed into timeless 'history'.[5]

This view is based on the abstraction of something purely, and therefore eternally, 'artistic'. It attributes to 'Art' a quality which adheres or does not adhere to an object, as if it were an entity instead of a function. In actual history, objects operate or cease to operate as works of art. There is no intrinsic quality called 'Art' which makes them operative. The view of art as eternal, as a once given universal, is not a view shared by historians, it is the view peculiar to the aesthetic interpreter. It reminds one of the religious approach, where it is not the object of admiration which is wonderful but the faith of the believer which is miraculous.

The work of art is made by an artist who lives in social space and social time. The work of the artists can only be understood by following or repeating the creation of their imagination which, like ours, is rooted in social life. The distinction between the artist and the spectator has to be abandoned for our analysis. The assumption that artists create from a different knowledge or a different world from our own must be given up. By breaking down the distinction between artistic life and life, between work and 'creation', by revealing the mystery not as a mystery but as a process of action, one comes nearer to the truth that artists are working men, not gods, and that their work can be understood.

By linking the manifestations of free will and free imagination to man's place in social life, one is brought into conflict with the self-conscious statements of some of the artists themselves and certainly with all the merchants of the supernatural, yet one need not adopt a form of materialist determinism, where cause and effect are so closely linked that no room is allowed for man's irrationality and fantasy. On the contrary, the interesting point is that freedom itself is determined, that the imagination obeys the laws of necessity in a reluctant, recalcitrant, yet wholly convincing form. Even man's proudest freedom, that of thought and fantasy, is less free than his illusions allow. Even his dreams are dreamt in the straitjacket of social reality. To some this may be a discouraging thought, to others reassurance that man in his maddest moments remains sane, because the fetters of social life bind him to nature and reality.

The work of art has always had a function, but there is a difference in its importance when it is an absolute necessity in a cult or, as appears from the Renaissance onwards, a desirable decoration with many layers of meaning: instructive, moral, civic, religious or personal, as part of the self-definition of man and his actions, still strongly linked with spiritual and social life, discussed, compared, criticised, praised and valued according to developing canons of artistic theories.

It is not accidental that art criticism and a purely aesthetic approach originate with the new function of the work of art itself. When art is a necessity there are no art critics, and not even the artist doubts the value of his own existence. Since the Renaissance the work of art has gained in self-importance in the same proportion as it has lost its *raison d'être*. The more the work of art is praised and discussed, the more suspicious one becomes of its relevance to anything but its own existence. The world of art then arises, and its members, the artists and theorists, the connoisseurs and collectors, the dealers and the critics, make their appearance. The world of art develops its own discourse and reflects more and more the fashions of the educated mind.

Leonardo in his 'Paragone' argues that painting is an activity of thought and should be considered like poetry. He claims that artists are men of letters and should be treated as such. The manual work entailed was not as important as the thought and knowledge of the artist. Painting became scientific with the mathematical skills needed for perspective construction. The artist became, as Leonardo clearly saw, a member of the liberal professions, like a poet, a doctor, a lawyer, a writer. His labour conditions had escaped the guild regulations; he was now free to work and ask any price for his individual wares. The question whether art is an independent activity now seems to emerge. From the Renaissance onwards the illusion that the work of the artist is an independent activity spreads, but the actual answer is that the activity of the artist now becomes a dependent activity in a subtler and more complex way; we are reaching the modern problem.

The concept of art has to be distinguished clearly from the work of art as such. The work had a real meaning and a social role to fulfil; works of art were nearer to what traffic signs are today, directing posts to right thinking and action. The aesthetic qualities of a traffic sign are quite high, but we look at it for information and reassurance – that is what it has in common with an altarpiece. The free artist in a free-market society has become an individual free agent who has to make decisions of a practical commercial and moral nature. The artist now becomes dependent on his customers – be they still called patron or buyer – like doctors and poets. He is now selling his skills and gifts, not only his craft but also his ideas. Hence the beginning of the concept of genius and 'thought' as a saleable commodity on the market. It is only from the sixteenth century onwards, parallel with the new market economy, that the concept of the individual artist develops; his uniqueness and his work is distinguished by his originality and not by his conformity.

Throughout the eighteenth and nineteenth centuries the exhibition, as known today, developed. In the exhibition the artist for the first time meets his public. The nineteenth-century exhibition presents the new social role of the work of art as a merchandise, in conformity with the creation of a competitive market economy. The artist has to enter the same social relations; his product now is competitive and he exhibits in the market. What he has to sell is his own creation, his own personality, his uniqueness. He had aimed at a generalised statement of a world view; he now has to aim at a different state of awareness and representation. In that new process of thought the old limitations of the pictorial convention had to be broken down, because the convention had been designed and agreed for an objective aim. While the new artist will aim at a conceptual art, which owes everything to him, the modern picture would not and cannot be bound by the pictorial conventions of the past, because the pictorial forms are a language and the new ideas could not be expressed by a convention of signs which was inadequate for the new content. The changed state of the artist had to lead to a changed state of the picture; the changes within the picture frame are caused by the changes in the frame of mind of the artists, and the formal problems of modern painting cannot be divorced from the informal problems of the artist's consciousness of his role. This is not the same question as that of the social role or function of the artist, but a different question, about the reflection or distortion of that problem within the artist himself, and the way in which he tried to solve it in his work.

The statement then is: that at the moment when the *content* of the work of art has lost its traditional ideological function the *forms* of the work of art become the new ideology.

The question of ideology was hardly relevant when society had one overriding set of assumptions. An Egyptian or a Christian artist had no conscience to square; he worked in a unified process of thought and production. The change in the meaning of the word 'Art' arose at the time when art ceased to be the carrier of an ideology, became detached as 'Art', and as such became its own ideology. Thereafter it was used as art, as an ideological prop of the ruling class.

There are thus three ideological levels in the work of art:

The *out*spoken ideology of what it stood for in its own time, and the honest reason for which it was made.

The *un*spoken or hidden ideology, which it betrays without knowing it – the 'false consciousness', as Marx would say.

Its ideological use as an 'Art' object, its presentation, ownership and the level of 'culture' it defines. In that category it becomes a token; the knowledge of it and its value alone determine its place in the social situation. This third level is, then, knowledge of art as a cultural, social asset, the possession of which defines rank.

The artist himself was active in the pictorial revolution, which entailed not just the breakdown of the formal tradition, but also the restructuring of the relation between form and content within the picture, and this new function of the work of art presents in itself an ideological change, which will become more and more visible to the public as well as to the artist.

The fundamental change which the artist underwent was his changing attitude towards reality; the positive facts of a given visible world are no more his main concern, but the search for the content of reality is within himself. Artists speak about *their* art, not in the sense of skill, but in the sense of fulfilment of their inner vision. They want to externalise the images they carry in their mind – they usually prefer the word soul. Again, this is not their whim or a pose, but their response to an actual situation. The illusions which man uses to disguise his social condition to himself are translated into a new reality – the work of art. In the process of fleeing from the visible world, a new world is created which becomes visible. The artist is then forced to create objective reality in the very process of denying it. This process may be defined as the dialectics of negation, where the escape becomes the arrival.

The very first demand made by the new artist was that the picture itself was to be treated as autonomous, it had to obey no laws but those of itself and its law-giver, the painter. All demands of realism, naturalism, anecdotalism, were rejected; all compositional rules, all rules of good behaviour of form and colour, were discarded and with Gauguin the march towards abstraction begins. Although to us his paintings are still emotionally and spiritually heightened pictures of a recognisable world, all the demands for, and all the elements of, 'pure' painting had been set.

The artist's preoccupation is with the state of art, the meaning of art. The artist's individual struggle to save himself and his art are the unconscious responses to the threat in social reality. By stating the problem in this manner, that man is reacting within and against a social framework, one does not detract from the struggles and victories of the artist.

In the process of changing the pictorial form, a whole new aesthetic arose which had its roots in the ideas of society. How the rediscovery of the primitive and the naïve was transmuted by the painters to account for the new choice of subject-matter and the complete disappearance of the object is the development of modern art. There appear in the imagination of the West what can only be called monsters, if seen under the aesthetic of the past; masks and primitive images make their appearance for the first time in European painting. Already in the nineteenth century the process of reappraisal of the past had begun. The European aesthetic was changing from the classical ideal. From mid-century onwards a reappraisal of simplicity and strength, of primitive vision and hieratic earnestness develops in opposition to the art of the Salon. Gauguin opposed refined art to primitive art, and stated: 'Primitive art stems from the spirit . . . so-called fine art from sense impressions.'[6] One can already hear the voices of the twentieth century: '. . . the greatest skill of the brush can only hurt a work of the imagination, because it emphasizes the material.'[7]

In this search for new expressive forms, the modern artist travelled over the whole range of the world of art. It was the modern artist who looked back, not the Stone Age which looked forward. The point he will reach is the autonomous picture, the painting which has no other intention but to be itself, not intending to depict anything. The autonomous artist will create the autonomous picture.

This liberation of painting was a social and moral necessity; it arose when the painter had begun to think about his role in life. He had gone out of social and private service, he was a free man. He could either deplore his loss of servitude and do his best to please, or he could, as some did, proclaim that art itself was his salvation, that through his service to art he would serve mankind. This moral and missionary theme is a recurring thread in the statements of the modern artist. With the changed position of the artist, the visual means with which he operates also change. This process is clear neither to him nor to his public, yet the artist, by a form of necessity which he interprets as his own, forces the picture to answer new demands. In that process the pictorial elements also liberate themselves from the older forms of necessity, until at the end of the century they are found to have become the available tools for an art form which can break completely with tradition.

'Being determines consciousness';[8] that consciousness, however, does not mirror the social being directly, but reflects the state in which consciousness becomes the awareness of the individual. The artist could choose to become an outsider and the clown, or the saviour and prophet of his own art. We shall see that both these roads found their travellers and that in both cases the actual social question is hidden from the artists' vision. Both roads are roads of despair, one sarcastic, the other sacramental.

As documentary evidence of the artist's awareness of his changing social position, the response of the artists themselves can be quoted in the form of pictures as quotations, beginning with Velazquez' painting of *The Maids of Honour* of the Spanish Royal family (Plate 1). This much discussed painting raises many problems, but we are concerned only with one, that of the painter himself, standing at his easel, the equal of the king who watches the scene. Velazquez is the master because he is in command and though he serves the court, at this moment the court obeys his command to stand still. It is the highest point of the artist's social role, a trusted friend of the king, conscious of his own worth and knowing that he is respected by the highest in the land. This was in the middle of the seventeenth century. In the middle of the eighteenth century, Hogarth paints himself as a private citizen at work, c. 1757 (Plate 2). At the same time, Reynolds paints himself as a young genius, 1753–54 (Plate 3), and later in 1773–80, as the President of the Royal Academy facing his public (Plate 4). In the last year of the century, in 1799, Goya draws the painter as a portraitist (Plate 5), but the proud master has become an ironical monkey, still the servant of the aristocracy, but already the joker about his own fate. Ten years after the French Revolution, Goya's engraving shows doubts not only about the aristocracy, but also about the position of the artist. Daumier takes up the question in the nineteenth century. He sees the artist as Don Quixote, a pathetic and lovable figure of heroic defeatism: see

Plate 1. Diego Rodriguez Velazquez: The Royal Family ('Las Meninas') 1656
Oil on canvas 318 × 276 cm. *Museo del Prado, Madrid*

Don Quixote Reading of 1865–67 (Plate 6), together with *The Artist
Sitting before his Work* of 1863–66 (Plate 7). The identification of
Don Quixote and the artist is Daumier's own. Daumier takes up the
theme with the outcasts of his own society, the artist, the mountebank,

15

Plate 2. William Hogarth: Self Portrait *c.*1757
Oil on canvas 39·4 × 37·4 cm. *National Portrait Gallery, London*

the street singer, and it is exactly this idea which Picasso takes up
with his saltimbanques and his circus people, the pure artist living solely
for his art, the outcast, the entertainer, the clown, a very romantic
and a very honest statement, expressed clearly in the *Mountebanks
Changing Place*, *c.* 1867, by Daumier (Plate 8), and *Family of Saltimbanques*, 1905, by Picasso (Plate 9).

The artist identifies the outcasts with himself; he is not using the world
of the circus and the street-players as subject-matter, he is using it to

symbolise the role of the artist and the entertainer in the world. The artist as clown will be a recurring portrayal of the painter, in Rouault, in Beckmann, in Heckel, and above all in Picasso's own work. There is no clearer pictorial proof of the artist's doubt about his role than when he shows himself as entertainer or fool. This new awareness of the artist has, however, another side and that is the moral side; the artist as a lost soul not only wants to save his own soul, but sees himself as a prophet and saviour. Two pictorial documents are the *Dying Pierrot* by Erich Heckel (Plate 10), an etching of 1913, of which there was also a painting. This composition is a lamentation over the dead Christ with the Three Marys in their traditional place. Another representation of the artist as saviour is Gauguin's *Self Portrait with Halo* (Plate 11). The problem of the artist's identity, his role as clown or Christ, his use of the mask and the use he will make of the interplay between the mask and the persona, can be read from the many paintings which deal with the subject. They all point to the inner state of the artist in his new role. As a painter he has in his work to express himself in a new situation. In his approach to the picture, as well as in the resulting formal composition, the artist reveals his new position and his new concerns.

Looking at some of the works which have preceded the twentieth century, we understand the magnitude of the pictorial revolution which the twentieth century has brought about. The distinct discoveries of the Renaissance masters, which held their validity and which distinguished them from all previous painters, can be summarised as follows: the illusion of three-dimensional space; the illusion of volumes; the illusion of textures of materials; the accuracy of anatomy and bodily movements; the accuracy of local colour, a technical term to describe the actual colour of the object. The technical means which the artists had developed to accomplish these aims had been: central or linear perspective where the lines of sight converge on one point; the perspective of colour or aerial perspective, when it was observed that distant objects were seen in different colours to those observed at close range; modelling of volumes with light and shade, thereby creating the sensation of being able to feel the textures of objects, grasp the volumes, the space, the distances, the reality of everything depicted. Jan van Eyck's *Madonna with the Canon van der Paele* of 1436 in Bruges (Plate 12) is sufficient to illustrate all the points enumerated: the perspective unity, the tactile qualities of volumes and textures, the unified lighting, the modelling with light and shade. All these achievements are based on empirical observation of the actual world around them. These discoveries were only possible in a social and spiritual climate which made the acceptance and observation of the material world possible.

Plate 3. Sir Joshua Reynolds: Self Portrait 1753–54
    Oil on canvas 63·5 × 74·1 cm. *National Portrait Gallery, London*

Between the fifteenth and the nineteenth centuries there was no break
in the spatial convention, and the most 'modern' artists of the nineteenth
century, the Impressionists, never questioned the space of the picture.
The Impressionists are in truth the last group of painters in the Renaissance tradition; in fact, they are not the forerunners of the new art,
but the last of the Renaissance. They not only respect, but improve
upon some of the Renaissance discoveries. Some suggestions on coloured
shadows first made by Leonardo are only taken up by the Impressionists.
In every respect they observe linear perspective, aerial perspective,
volume, texture, light and shadow. They have refined the means; they
add only one new aim, that is, a conscious concentration on the fleeting
truth as opposed to the Renaissance aim of a more formalised, lasting,
ideal truth. In comparing Impressionist paintings with post-Renaissance

Plate 4. Sir Joshua Reynolds: Self Portrait 1773–80
Oil on canvas 127 × 101·6 cm. *Royal Academy of Arts, London*

Plate 5. Francisco de Goya y
Lucientes:
Etching 20 × 15 cm., *Los
Caprichos* 1799, pl. 41,
British Museum, London

Plate 6. Honoré Daumier: Don Quixote Reading 1865–67
Oil on panel 33·6 × 26 cm. *National Gallery of Victoria, Melbourne*

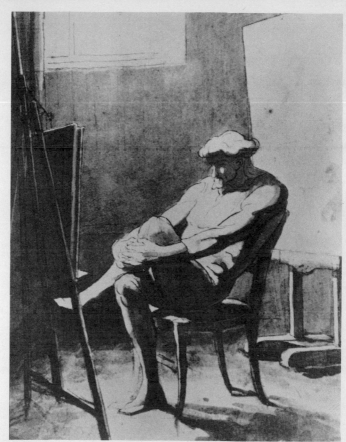

Plate 7. Honoré Daumier: The Artist sitting before his Work 1863–66
Pen and sepia wash 38 × 29 cm. *Private Collection, Paris*

paintings, the adherence of the Impressionists to the space convention can be seen. The fundamental concepts were never placed in doubt: *A Money Changer and his Wife* of 1512 by Quentin Massys (Plate 13) and *L'Absinthe* of 1876 by Degas (Plate 14). What the Impressionists achieved for the last time was to fill the old formulas with new life. By an honest and lively representation of bourgeois life, by their positive acceptance of the world around them, they had set themselves apart from those Salon and Academy pictures which were so markedly dishonest and discredited. The revolution of the twentieth century was not directed against the Academy any more, it was directed towards overcoming the limitations of the optical picture. It was to be a break in the forms and functions of the work of art.

The new artists were aiming at the creation of a new and pure art, an art directly concerned with the transformation of their vision and experience which did not obey the optical laws that all previous artists

21

Plate 8. Honoré Daumier: Mountebanks Changing Place *c*. 1867
        Black, red and white crayon with ink washes on cream paper 36·1 × 27·9 cm.
        Wadsworth Atheneum, Hartford

Plate 9. Pablo Picasso: Family of Saltimbanques 1905
Oil on canvas 212·8 × 229·6 cm. *National Gallery of Art, Washington, D.C.*

Plate 10. Erich Heckel: Dying Pierrot 1912
Etching 15·4 × 11·4 cm. *Mrs Siddy Heckel*

Plate 11. Paul Gauguin: Self Portrait with Halo 1889
Wood panel 79 × 52 cm. *National Gallery of Art, Washington, D.C.,
Chester Dale Collection*

Plate 12. Jan van Eyck: Madonna with the Canon van der Paele 1436
Panel 122 × 157 cm. *Groeninge Museum, Bruges*

had respected. They thus came into conflict with their own traditions which they intended to overthrow, and in this process they overthrew the conventions of perspective space. Not what they saw, but what they felt and what they knew was to be expressed in their pictures. The condition of the picture had not changed, the artist was still confined to a flat surface with four corners. Thus one has to observe the similarities between the new and the old, and at the same time become aware of the great innovations. Even a pictorial revolution must leave some conditions unchanged, and it will be essential to grasp the importance of the new within the shattering framework of the old.

Gauguin's *Three Tahitians* of 1899 (Plate 15) is a clearly readable and in itself simple and decorative picture. There is no real distance; the figures stand more towards the front, and there is a background, or back-cloth, but the distance is indistinct and of no importance. Space has been lost, though the figures are in definite relations of size and scale and to our trained eye, neither awkward to read nor difficult to disentangle (at the time when the picture was painted it was different). Yet something important has happened. The scene is more in your mind than before you. You cannot really enter the picture space. In this Gauguin there is no distance in the picture, but a big distance between us and the picture. The picture will become more and more enclosed and isolated, until it becomes quite hermetic.

The modern picture moves away from the world and encloses its content, so to say, behind closed windows. We can still see what happens, but can no longer see the things themselves, only their signs and symbols which we can rethink and reconstitute. What we see is not any more a mirror of life or thought, but something less visual, less tangible and more conceptual

In the *Dance* of 1909 by Matisse (Plate 16) the picture becomes a *locus* which has its own laws, which are not those of the natural space which remained the condition of any action in the picture. Perspective is not respected, aerial perspective is abandoned, anatomical accuracy has gone, local colour is given up, there is still a near and a far, but it is no longer the replica or the mirror of anything; it is itself alone, with its elements of line and colour-making shapes. These shapes no longer have to obey any spatial laws. They are now divorced from all necessity to describe recession, light, shadow, volumes. The fact that the shapes and colours still indicate recognisable objects in a recognisable setting are not the important points of the argument. The argument is that these lines or colours could just as well do other things.

The spectator can enter a Renaissance painting. He can walk mentally into and move within that mirror image of reality; the spaces, the views, the horizons are all his. He can become a traveller in the picture. Not so in a medieval painting, where he was face to face not with an extension of his world, but with a different world. There he could read the symbols and understand them, but he was not part of the event, nor was he meant to be. When the modern artist in our century overthrows the Renaissance concepts of space and illusion, he thereby prevents us from participating in the world of the picture. He expels us from the work of art and returns us to the position of the pre-Renaissance spectator who faced a conceptual art, not of the eye, but of the mind.

This return to a conceptual art, abandoning all optical illusions on which painting had depended, was achieved with revolutionary speed. The autonomous world of the picture is established. The autonomy of the picture, the fundamental novelty of modern art, has been achieved when the artist has expelled the spectator from direct participation in the picture. It is the artist's response to the public which had expelled the painter from social life.

Plate 13. Quentin Massys: A Money Changer and his Wife 1514
Panel 71 × 68 cm. *Musée du Louvre, Paris*

Plate 14. Edgar Degas: L'Absinthe 1876
Oil on canvas 92 × 68 cm. *Musée du Jeu de Paume, Paris*

29

Plate 15. Paul Gauguin: Three Tahitians 1899
Oil on canvas 73 × 94 cm. *National Gallery of Scotland, Edinburgh*

2

Space and Time

Out of the new social situation of the artist, a multitude of rational-isations and theoretical statements arose which are all different guises for the fundamental fact that the artist was on his own and had to dis-cover for himself his own road towards his self-realisation as an artist. This self-realisation was accompanied by theoretical or pseudo-theoreti-cal statements. In this chapter the Cubist and Futurist theories – both theories of 'reality' – will be considered.

In considering the theories and ideas behind a work of art, one has to distinguish between what is theory before the act and what is interpre-tation after the act. It is erroneous to assume that an artist has thoughts and ideas which he paints into a picture. There is no such translation. His ideas and thoughts are motivating directives, faintly or strongly felt, hardly ever precisely understood. They are the springs for action and they are a code which the artist tries to translate into a pictorial form. But that code – it may be derived from a reading of a Dostoievsky novel, or a misunderstanding of Bergson's philosophy – is not the code in which the novel or the philosophy could be expressed. It is the artist's own shorthand summary, imbued with his own conceptions and mis-conceptions. It becomes his theory or intention, and it need have very little to do with the original source. The artist manufactures his mumbo-jumbo out of the *bricolage* of his life and emotions and the social reality in which he lives. There is no direct causation, there is no order and there is no straight line, and yet this odd mixture is his own, and out of that pool of ideas and images something arises which is the work of art. He is an individual, yet he is more and less than that. In the words of Sartre from his lengthy study on Flaubert, *L'Idiot de la Famille*: 'A man is never an individual', but rather 'a universal singular, completed and universalised by his period, which he completes by producing himself within that period in his singularity.'[9] In the actual process of painting the struggle is fought out with the picture's own pictorial problems. It is a two-way process: the artist has a hope and an intention. The picture already has its own rights and its own intentions. That pro-cess of birth or creation is a struggle between pictorial necessity and artistic intention. The painting teaches the artist as much as the artist teaches the painting. Between a straight reading of the artist's philosophy

31

Plate 16. Henri Matisse: Dance 1909
  Oil on canvas 260·6 × 389·2 cm. *Museum of Modern Art, New York, gift of Nelson A. Rockefeller in honour of Alfred H. Barr, Jr.*

and the reading of the picture's existence, falls the shadow of the picture itself, which is in every case different from the philosophy from which it arose, not only because there is no code of translation, but also because the picture itself has taken part in the act of creation. The artist himself knows it. 'Braque always said that the only thing that counts, in painting, is the intention, and it's true,' says Picasso. 'What counts is what one wants to do, and not what one does. That's what's important. In Cubism, in the end what was important is what one *wanted* to do, the intention one had. And *that* one cannot paint.'[10] So according to the painter the important thing, the intention, cannot be painted. Yet he does paint pictures and though they must fall short of his intention, there are still traces of the intention and these we are able to discern. What the artist always has had to do was to find a transcript for contemporary reality. What was placed in doubt at the beginning of the twentieth century was exactly the unchanging stable nature of material reality.

The physical world picture at the beginning of the twentieth century was undergoing its greatest revolution since Newton. All the well-established assumptions of the nature of space and time were challenged by the new physics. When the painter had achieved an absolutely perfect rendering of the material world, that very world of objective observation was placed in doubt. The artists reacted to this doubt with their own means within the world of the picture. They destroyed the old conventional reality and, in the process of destroying the pictorial language, gave expression to newer concepts of reality. One can read between the lines of the picture the serious questions and intentions of the artist. In the year 1905, Einstein published his first paper *The Special Theory of Relativity*, and in 1906 Picasso painted his *Demoiselles d'Avignon*, his first Cubist picture. These acts are independent; there is not the slightest reason to assume that Einstein then knew who Picasso was, or had seen any of his pictures. Nor is it likely that Picasso had read the Einstein paper, or has done so later. But what the two shared was living in the same world, and what they both did in their very separate ways and different modes of expression was very simply one thing: they both detached the observer from his fixed position. In Einstein's case, the observer from the physical universe, in Picasso's case, the observer, usually called the spectator, from the picture.

Around 1900, at the beginning of the artistic revolution, the artist began to experiment, to treat his picture not as an interpretation of the visible world in the traditional sense, but as a possibility. Without this experimental approach to the picture, modern art and its history would not be explicable. Cubism is the most experimental and fruitful development of the early years of modern art, that is, the period 1905–12.

Einstein wrote that 'it became more and more evident that Classical mechanics affords an insufficient foundation for the physical description of all natural phenomena'.[11]

A system of co-ordinates is only valid as long as it remains '*equivalent for the description of natural phenomena*'.[12] A very similar way of thinking can be established for painting; a system of co-ordinates, in this case linear perspective, became inadequate. If at one point in history this old system of co-ordinates ceases to be a valid equivalent for the description of natural phenomena, or, in the case of painting, to be insufficient for the material and experience an artist can describe, then a new system of co-ordinates will have to be created which fulfils the needs of the artist, one which can contain the equivalents for the description of the phenomena he wishes to describe. Modern art begins when central perspective is abandoned and events happen in the picture which could not have been seen from one static point of view. So we are faced with the coincidence that at one and the same time a system of co-ordinates is questioned as valid by painters and by physicists. While one might recognise formal similarities – in their modes of thinking – which might link the Cubists with modern scientific thought, this must not confuse the issue of their different intentions. Scientists invent laws as a means of interpreting an actual, if complex, reality. Artists create from that reality something which we have to interpret.

The aim of the Cubists was that of a *conceptual* art, not an *optical* art. Their aim was not to paint what they saw, but to paint what they knew. Maurice Raynal in 1913 defined it quite clearly: 'The Primitives', then the term used for pre-Renaissance painters, 'obeyed a mysticism which illuminated their thinking . . . the Primitives *thought* rather than *painted* their pictures, and so they worked in accordance with that remarkable idea, of painting one's *conception*. . . . Instead of painting the objects as they saw them, they painted them as they thought them.'[13] So far so good, but now Raynal introduces an odd note: 'It is,' he says, 'precisely this law that the Cubists have readopted, amplified and codified under the name of "The Fourth Dimension".'[14] The term sounds familiar, but the meaning here is obscure. It is a first warning not to use terms in physics *and* in painting, as if they could possibly mean the same thing. Raynal, however, supplies an answer and possibly a true, or at least revealing one. 'The Cubists, not having the mysticism of the Primitives as a motive for painting, took from their own age a kind of mysticism of logic, of science and of reason, and this they have obeyed . . .'[15] What the Cubist painters and, much more, their poetic satellites had concocted was a myth called the fourth dimension which had nothing in common with the scientific use of the term and yet served as their justification or rationalisation of what they were doing. One has to distinguish clearly between the actual doings of the artists, that is, the paintings which are not out of tune with the new scientific concepts, and the terminology used, false of course, in which they became aware of what they were doing in a distorted form. In his *Méditations Esthétiques: Les Peintres Cubistes*, of 1913,[16] Guillaume Apollinaire also talks about Cubism and the fourth dimension. Apollinaire is an important figure in the history of Cubism; he was a very close friend of the Cubist painters, but Picasso has often stated that Apollinaire had nothing to do with the inception of Cubism, and that his theories are of as little value as any other. Picasso is no doubt right, but if we wish to accept nothing from Apollinaire, we have to accept nevertheless that he was there and that his thoughts, or even his gossip, are strictly contemporary and connected with the artists.

Apollinaire formulates the dialectical sentence that 'artists are men who want to become non-human (*inhumain*). They search . . . for traces of non-humanity, traces which one cannot find in nature. Those traces are the truth and outside them we cannot know any reality.'[17] This is then an argument that the artists have abandoned painting nature in the sense of visible reality and are probing into the laws of the structure of nature and that an entirely new art will arise. 'Today,' Apollinaire says, 'the scientists do not confine themselves to the three dimensions of Euclidean geometry. Naturally and by intuition the painters were also led to the point where they concern themselves with new means of extension, which in the language of the modern studio is called the *fourth dimension.* . . . Let us add, that this imagining of a *fourth dimension* was for many young painters only a general expression of their searching, when they looked at Egyptian, oceanic or negro sculpture, or when they considered the writings of scientists, waiting for the arrival of a sublime art; and today one cannot retain this utopian concept, which had to be noted and explained anything more than its historic interest.'[18] This is a very subtle truth as stated by Apollinaire; the fourth dimension was a Utopian concept to be experienced in the future. From this we can at least be certain that the question of a fourth dimension was studio talk and, no matter how wrongly understood in the scientific sense, the artists had become aware that they were not living in the old world any more.

Alexandre Mercerau, though less well known than Apollinaire, also played an important role in the history of Cubist theory. He writes in 1914: 'Our artists ardently desire to achieve an integral truth as . . . today's art seeks to discover ultimate laws, more profound than those of yesterday. But just as the principles postulated by Bolyai, Lobatschevsky, Riemann, Beltrami and de Tilly have not destroyed those of Euclid, but merely relegated them to their true status as one postulate among many . . . the modern painter does not presume to negate everything accomplished before his time.'[19] This suggests a non-Euclidean geometry as a basis for Cubism. As early as 1905, Mecireas Goldberg, a little-known Polish Anarchist and art critic in Paris writing about an artist (Rouveyre) said: 'In these works there are visions of heads, shoulders, arms and joints that seemed to have escaped from Euclid's immortal book . . .'[20]

In discussing an art form and not a science, it may be appropriate to quote Apollinaire writing on Braque as early as 1908 and consider that, though Apollinaire had been talking about the fourth dimension and new science, he wrote: 'Let no-one expect to find here . . . [in the work of Braque] the psychology of the men of letters or the demonstrative logic of the scientists. This painter composes his pictures in absolute devotion to complete newness. . . . His canvases have a unity which renders them inevitable. To the painter, to the poet, to all artists – and this is what distinguishes them from other men, especially from the scientists – each work becomes a new universe with its own laws.'[21] That the artistic manifestations of a period are in line with the scientific need not surprise us.

The concept of space should now be clarified. The Renaissance had introduced Euclidean space into the picture, thus abandoning the non-physical, purely spiritual space of the Middle Ages; the three-dimensional picture space was a continuation of the space of the observer. The spectator stood outside the frame at an appropriate distance, calculated by the artist, and could look into and become part of that spatial organisation. Jan van Eyck's *Madonna* (Plate 12) stands as the perfect example of the Renaissance space conception. Whatever the artist painted was painted from one point of view and the spectator could enter the picture. The more realistic art became, the easier it was made for the spectator to enter a world he knew. One has to understand a dialectical process which was clearly foreseen by no less a dialectical thinker than Hegel himself. Hegel, in his *Phenomenology of the Spirit*, 1807, suggests that knowledge aims to become absolute knowledge. 'In his lectures on aesthetics he describes art and science as two forms of expression of the same need, the interpretation of the world and of life. At first he says Art has attempted to interpret the chaotic and opaque phenomena of the world, until at last science breaks through the mythical barrier and begins to answer the questions of mankind.'[22] Hegel wrote: 'Thought and reflection have outdistanced art. . . . Art does not any more satisfy our mental needs, which earlier periods and peoples have sought and found in art and in art only.'[23] 'For a time thereafter, art and science were equal, until science surpassed art.'[24] Hegel, more advanced even than Marx, says: 'The beautiful days of

Greek art, as well as the golden middle ages, are over . . .'[25] Hegel was aware that the equality of art and science in the interpretation of the world had come to an end. The artist himself now lives with a scientific world picture (or often with a deliberately anti-scientific world picture), but in either case reacts to it. The triad, then, is art as the thesis, antithesis to science, and the various syntheses which the artists attempt. That in the process the synthesis, the work of art, destroys the thesis and the antithesis, is only good and proper dialectics.

Braque and Picasso met in 1907 through Apollinaire. In 1906–7 Picasso had already painted his famous *Les Demoiselles d'Avignon* (Plate 17). In this proto-Cubist picture, from which art historians date the inception of Cubism, we encounter the problems of Cubism. Apollinaire wrote: 'In representing the conceived reality or the created reality, the artist can give the appearance of the three dimensions, he can, in a way "cubicise" (*cubiquer*) . . . which would deform the quality of the conceived or created form.'[26]

There are no theoretical statements by either Picasso or Braque. Braque has written about the secrets in art, but much later and he does not deal with theory. Picasso has, very deliberately, avoided all theoretical statements, and both have on many occasions declared that the writings of Apollinaire, as well as the theories of Metzinger, had nothing to do with their work. When, during the Cubist adventure, anyone tried to ask questions of Picasso, his reply was: 'Il est défendu de parler au pilote'.[27] The truth, of course, is that no artist, or very few artists, work in accordance with a theory and yet all their work conforms to an intention, and it is those intentions which the theorists can analyse with more or less success.

Apollinaire writes in *Méditations Esthétiques: Les Peintres Cubistes:* 'What distinguishes Cubism from traditional (*ancienne*) painting, is that it is not an art of imitation but an art of conception, which tends to raise itself towards creation.'[28] A conceptual art assembles its elements in the process of forming a picture of a reality not hitherto existing. The Cubist paints objects not from one point of view at a time, but from several points of view to give us simultaneous views of the object. It is as if artist and observer are moving around and stand above and below and even within the object at the same time. What the Cubists achieve is the destruction of linear perspective, which presupposes the static observer, and they take the spectator into the picture space from where alone mentally he could adjust his mind to the sum of disparate perspectives which assail him.

A drawing by Picasso (Plate 18) are studies of the same glass from all sides, from the top, from the bottom and sideways and in that process we see the different aspects from a plain circle to an unrecognisable

Plate 17. Pablo Picasso: Les Demoiselles d'Avignon 1907
Oil on canvas 244 × 233 cm. *Museum of Modern Art, New York, acquired through the Lillie P. Bliss Bequest*

conic section combined. A very similar drawing, *Still Life with Glass, Bottle and Playing Card* (Plate 19) shows the almost systematic destruction of central perspective. Here is a complete picture where Cubist internal perspectives combining the different aspects of objects is completed. The forms are distorted in the sense that they combine several single views of undistorted forms in one image. This process can be observed in *Still Life with Chocolate Pot* of 1909 (Plate 20). The aim of

37

Plate 18. Pablo Picasso: Studies of Glasses 1914–15
Pencil 24·7 × 31·7 cm. *Private Collection*

Cubism was the exploration of space in the forms of solid objects. In this process perspective was dissolved, or rather, multiplied. The observer was no longer fixed in the one place from which alone the picture under linear perspective looks true. The painter combines in one picture many view-points and illuminates space from many sides, including the positions from within the picture space itself. The spectator thus ceases to be mentally at rest and is taken within the system of the picture where mentally he changes view-points, and is in a form of movement around, through, above and below the newly created reality. The Cubist painter makes us enter an Alice Through the Looking Glass world.

That Braque and Picasso thought alike and worked in the same spirit is seen in *Violin et Cruche* by Braque, 1910 (Plate 21). In Cubism, the planes within the picture which interpenetrate each other create spatial relations which defy rational solutions and yet preserve and deliberately enhance the two-dimensionality of the picture itself. The paradox is,

38

Plate 19. Pablo Picasso: Still Life with Glass, Bottle and Playing Card 1913–14
Pencil 49·5 × 39 cm. *National Gallery, Prague*

then, that the Cubists refuse to create an illusion of space. They say, so
to speak, that anyone who thinks that linear perspective is true and can
enter the picture, is a fool; a picture is a flat, painted object, but within
it the artist can create spaces and dimensions which were not there before.
The picture is an artificial product and should not be mistaken for an
illusion of real space.

Having dealt with the Cubist approach to space and before coming to
the question of time, I shall make my own contribution to the confusion.
As we are already in the middle of a philosophical muddle, I wish to
raise the spectre of the nature of reality in art, because the Cubists have
also raised it.

There is one element in Cubism which may have some bearing on the
subject: this element is a paradoxical reversal of the old trick of the
painters, known as *trompe l'œil*, a term which defines the most illusionist
form of painting to deceive the eye. In that field all tricks of perspective
were used to such effect that the illusion was complete and the spectator

Plate 20. Pablo Picasso: Still Life with Chocolate Pot 1909
Watercolour 61·3 × 47·5 cm. *Private Collection*

was, to his delight, completely fooled. This trickery made much use of false shadows and careful imitation of surface texture. A wonderful example is *Le Vin* by y Llorente, seventeenth century (Plate 22), where not even all the tricks of the trade are used but where even the Cubists are anticipated. This is an example of the painter raising the problem of the painting as truth. He paints a picture with a painting in the picture and contrasts it to the painting of reality – also painted. The Cubists asked the same question, but with greater ruthlessness. They took reality to bits and stuck bits of it on to the painting. Instead of imitating newspaper, they stuck a real newspaper in the picture, but then went on to paint newspaper. To make confusion worse confounded, they stuck grained wood on to the canvas and then imitated grained wood. Braque must have thought of it, because he was originally a house decorator trained in graining and marbling, a favourite form of deception. In fact, the Cubists seem to say 'Don't trust your eyes, nothing is what it seems to be, all is trickery, it all depends on what you expect.' This

40

Plate 21. Georges Braque: Violin et Cruche 1910
Oil on canvas 117 × 73·5 cm. *Kunstmuseum, Basle*

Plate 22. German y Llorente: Nature Morte en Trompe l'Oeil Le Vin,
early eighteenth century
Oil on canvas 70 × 50 cm. *Musée du Louvre, Paris*

makes fun of the observer and, incidentally, traditional art. It is an intentional alienation of both art and the spectator; it helps further in the destruction of a stable and preconceived picture of the world and, at the same time, of a hitherto firmly held picture of the picture. The old master, Llorente, still painted both his picture and his reality; the Cubists make fun of both. *Still Life with Match Box* by Picasso (Plate 23) with a visiting card added makes it clear that the spectator is face to face with

Plate 23. Pablo Picasso: Still Life with Match Box
Charcoal drawing and collage 28 × 35 cm. *Private Collection*

two sorts of realities. The most perfect example, however, is the *Still Life on Cane Chair*, 1911–12 (Plate 24) where 'Art' so to say sits down in reality itself, so you are certain not to know who is crazy, you or the picture.

Picasso and Braque intended to make fun of reality in its old-

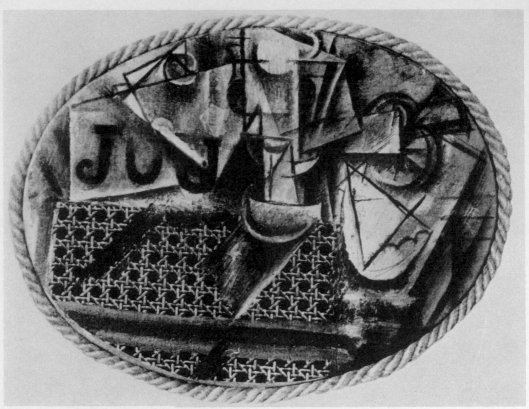

Plate 24. Pablo Picasso: Still Life on Cane Chair 1911–12
Oil, oilcloth and paper on canvas 27 × 35 cm. *Private Collection*

established, prerecognisable forms; they wanted to make the spectator aware that his attitude, the way he measures things for their reality content, or better, reality context, is part of the game. This, too, is a relativistic position where two concepts, the picture and the spectator, are placed in a new relationship. Much to the spectator's surprise, he is forced to abandon his assumptions. This is exactly what happened to the physicists with the theory of relativity; they had to abandon some cherished and valued assumptions and had to test new data by giving up old assumptions. It is this kind of parallel attitude which we find in the field of art and physics and which is significant for the climate of opinion at the beginning of the century.

Having considered the assembly of form derived from the object in its many aspects, one can also follow this development with the human form and, eventually, the moving body. A drawing by Picasso dating from 1912–13, *Head of a Man* (Plate 25), shows forms which are separated and analysed. This is the preliminary process of analysis of the body at rest; the human figure as an object in the picture, no more important than a mandolin. But a body can move and the problem of movement

44

has always occupied the painter. The figures were frozen in one moment of time, and although by a variety of devices a sensation of floating in space, or even an illusion of speed, was attempted, the floating angel or race horse was frozen in time and space. There are many treatises dealing with the choice of the dramatic point of action, how to make the gestures pregnant with significance, so that the action (and action means movement) can be seen. Yet the painter had to paint a still picture, where at best an indication of movement was given which the spectator could follow. The raised sword remained raised for centuries and never felled an enemy. Like every artistic convention, such gestures were accepted as an indication of real action.

With Cubism, the relationship between painter and object was destroyed. The Cubists did not paint the objects as seen from one point of view, but combined within the same picture several different views of the same object. They painted the object simultaneously as seen from several sides. They combined in one and the same picture different movements which could only be accomplished in a sequence of time; thus a 'before', a 'now', and an 'after' was combined in one image, showing the movement of a body in time by a combined sequence of events made visible. The Cubists included the element of time, but had to present it in the only two available dimensions of the picture plane. By including time, the known forms of objects at rest were deformed. A distortion was necessary because a body changing position does, in fact, become different with each successive movement and the attempt to paint the sequence of movement simultaneously must lead to a distortion in the combination of forms. The distorted forms in a Cubist picture are the result of considering the object or, what amounts to the same, the observer to be in motion. If the experience of this mobile observation is to be combined in the figure, the distortion is unavoidable, as the known, undistorted, form is the form of the object at rest. In a drawing of 1916, *Woman in an Armchair* (Plate 26), the problem is simplified and we see two positions, even two characters of the woman, simultaneously.

One can in Cubism speak of something which pictorially approaches the concept of curved space, only in the two-dimensional world of the picture it leads to curved forms. The washbasin in the *Woman washing her Feet*, 1946 (Plate 27) is seen at one and the same time by the woman washing her feet and by the spectator who sees in one form two aspects which cannot be seen from a single point of view. The curvature of the basin is not right in classical drawing, but it becomes right and necessary in Cubism. Equally, the bending figure of the woman gives a combined form of what the spectator might see and what the woman herself feels of her own form. If you can bend as low as that, you carry too much of your own back on your shoulders, and if you have one foot in a washbasin, the other one carries too much weight. If the foot looks too large for classical concepts, the truth is that it carries a greater mass and therefore looks and feels and is bigger. The whole leg which goes with this foot expresses in its form the same knowledge. Picasso paints something more, not only the visible event, but the physical forces which this event contains. It is thus unavoidable that these additional factors of the event must distort the accepted forms. Having understood this, a

Plate 25. Pablo Picasso: Head of a Man 1912–13
Collage 62 × 47 cm. *Galerie Louise Leiris, Paris*

picture like *Sleeping Girl*, 1941 (Plate 28) will become easy to read; the succession of movements of a sleeping girl result in this combined figure. An even more complex form is contained in *L'Aubade* of 1942 (Plate 29). This picture should not stand just as an example of a method or principle,

Plate 26. Pablo Picasso: Woman in an Armchair 1916
Pencil 31·1 × 23·1 cm. *Private Collection*

but as a picture, full of sad, comic, sinister overtones. Who plays which
mandolin, who plays which strings? The parallel in the theory of
relativity is expressed by Einstein in the following terms: 'That we have
not been accustomed to regard the world in this sense as a four-dimen-
sional continuum is due to the fact that in physics, before the advent of
the theory of relativity, time played a different and more independent
role, as compared with the space co-ordinates.'[29] All that can be said is
that classical painting as well as classical physics were content to picture
their objects at rest and that the upheaval caused by new interpretations
was equalled in both worlds. Old assumptions die hard and to consider
motion as normal and rest as abnormal was new in the world of painting
and in physics. It would be futile to claim that Cubism was in any way

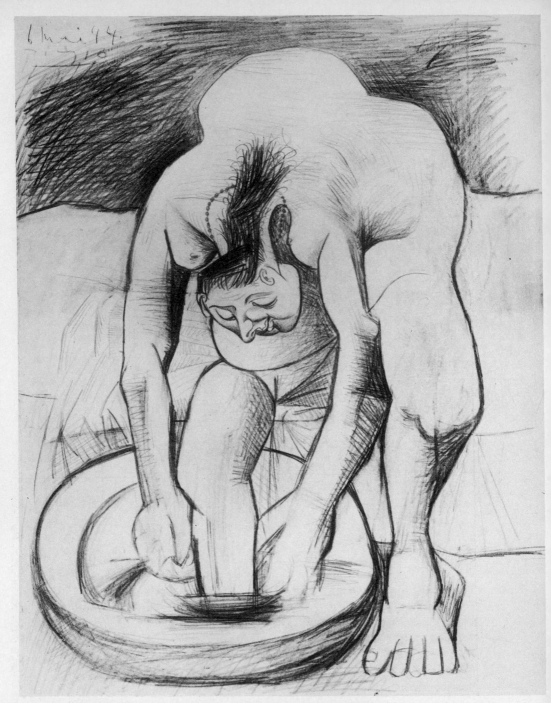

Plate 27. Pablo Picasso: Woman washing her Feet 1946
Pencil 51 × 38 cm. *Galerie Louise Leiris, Paris*

48

Plate 28. Pablo Picasso: Sleeping Girl 1941
Pencil 21 × 27 cm. *Galerie Louise Leiris, Paris*

Plate 29. Pablo Picasso: L'Aubade 1942
Oil on canvas 195 × 265 cm. *Musée National d'Art Moderne, Paris*

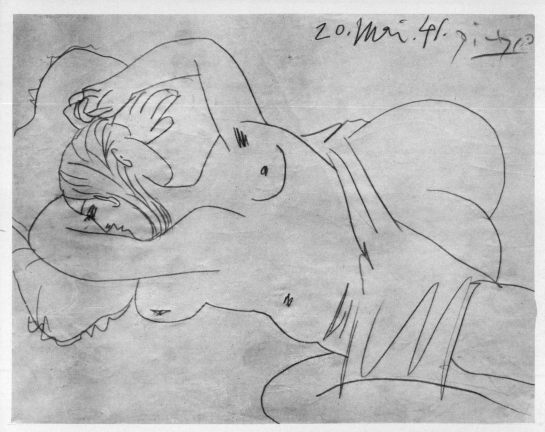

20. Mai. 41. Picasso

connected with Einstein's theories, or to prove that it was a necessary and unavoidable development in the art of painting. That it could not have been thought of at any other time in history is the only valid conclusion to be drawn from the coincidence. It was an experiment fruitful and revolutionary in painting, where it destroyed the optical and causal approach to the picture. That the painters for the first time attempted to paint not the moment of time but the relativity of time, that they introduced the mobile observer, are Cubist achievements.

A simple, everyday experience has to be considered. In the twentieth century speed was a new invention. You need a new sense of time and movement to jump clear of an automobile. Those who were most conscious of the new element in life – speed and light, movement and dynamism – were the Futurists. Their theoretical aim was to paint total knowledge of events in space and time. Boccioni meant that one should not paint just what one can see when standing still, but paint every thing one knows is there, in front, behind, above and below, one should paint simultaneously all that happens around one. The key word used again and again is simultaneity. Hence in Futurist painting an interpenetration of events, impinging upon each other and happening simultaneously as they actually do in the process of interpenetration, distort the forms. Futurism is a strange form of realism. The modern observer, sitting, let us say, on the top of a bus going round a corner, actually sees houses at odd angles; he sees cyclists disappearing under the bus, light reflections breaking in the glass panes, he has simultaneous experiences of many factors which he normally would try to suppress because he would become dizzy if he took it all in. But not before the physically fast-moving observer appeared did man have any experience of his surroundings passing almost too quickly for observation. Such obvious facts are rarely considered when talking about pictures. Painters on a motor-cycle see the world differently from artists on a walking tour through Wales. Futurism is the outcome of actual modern experience plus the intention of finding pictorial forms for that experience. *The Street penetrates the House*, 1911, by Boccioni (Plate 30) is one interpretation, Balla's *Speeding Automobile* of 1912 (Plate 31) another; here the new experience of the rapidly moving observer in a formerly static world is compressed.

Futurism attempts new means of depicting speed and dynamism. There was no dearth of innovation, a violent urge, but not a completely convincing solution. What is then a plausible explanation for the Futurist failure? The answer has been given by the Cubist discovery. The Futurists failed because they attempted to depict motion, but retained the concept of the static observer. The Futurist stands still and lets the world rattle by. In spite of the modern trappings, the fundamental

Plate 30. Umberto Boccioni: The Street penetrates the House 1911
Oil on canvas 100 × 100·6 cm. *Niedersächsisches Landesmuseum, Hanover*

concept is old-fashioned and out of tune with modern knowledge. It contains new sense impressions, but no new thought.

In *L'Atelier de la Modiste* of 1925 by Picasso (Plate 32) almost all the elements I have tried to separate come together. This perfect picture summarises all the achievements of Cubist organisation of time and space, and this is its triumph; it makes us feel already quite familiar with the experience we have gained. In fact, we have been transformed as much as the picture. The Cubists and the Futurists remain within the

51

Plate 31. Giacomo Balla: Speeding Automobile 1912
Oil on wood panel 55·8 × 68·5 cm. *Museum of Modern Art, New York*

empirical world and attempt an interpretation of events which constitute
that world. They are a new order of realists. All the arts are metaphorical; they give an equivalent of a state of mind as a picture of reality.
In the arts, assumptions find a form, be they literary or pictorial, yet
no picture or any work of art can be taken as an image of something
else. It is man himself who creates his universe for which he finds a
multitude of formal expressions. That such formal expressions have a
unity of style and awareness need not surprise one, because they are all
human and all are historical. We then postulate contemporaneity of the
mind as the sole ordering principle of the multitude of metaphorical
formulae in which the mind comes to terms with reality. As a materialist,
I am not denying the existence of physical reality; that reality is the
medium in which we exist and which man in his history transforms. Our
penetration of reality comprises all the assumptions of our modes of production under which it can be understood and all the aspects under

52

Plate 32. Pablo Picasso: L'Atelier de la Modiste 1925
Oil on canvas 172 × 265 cm. *Musée National d'Art Moderne, Paris*

which it manifests itself to our thought and our senses. Artists as well as scientists make discoveries which are valid as a human interpretation of events which, however, as events are in their own nature entirely other than the manifestations we observe, comprehend and make our own. The universe is versatile enough to be truthfully presented in many different forms; it can be approached by mathematical metaphors as well as by artistic metaphors. Going beyond the unity of physics, we could arrive at a new concept, which I would like to call the unity of metaphors, the structure which the historic mind derives from social reality.

3

The Artist as Conjurer

The autonomous artist of the twentieth century who lives his life consciously as an artist without a function, except the one he gives himself, lives in a state of symbiosis with his art. He creates it and it creates him. To the modern artist his work is the definition of his self. His life is the creation of his art. No one was more conscious of the fact that his private life was also his art than Picasso. He painted it as an autobiography.

In modern art one can very simply state that the content of the picture is the artist's intention; it is the painter's life, his will and his ego which forms the content of the picture. The rest of what we see, what was formerly called subject-matter, is only the incidental material with which he expresses his will. Picasso in his happy paradoxical way has said it as follows: 'The inner "I" is inevitably in my painting, since it is I who make it. I needn't worry about that. Whatever I do, it will be there. It will be all too much there. . . . It's the rest that is the problem!'[30] As the modern content is the artist, that leaves him only the task of solving the formal problems. As the formal solution of each picture is an individual choice of the artist and the content of the picture is the artist, one must be absolutely honest from the onset and say: 'If you don't like a man like Picasso and his way of being, you are not likely to like the way he expresses it, and every formal criticism you make will only be a rationalisation of *your* dislike.' The artist, by taking such a subjective view of the content of the picture, filling it completely with his own person, forces the spectator to take the same stand. He is forced to accept or reject the artist's work which is the artist's life *in toto*. There is no playing around with partial acceptances. A work by Picasso is the man – and he wanted it to be so. Thus every judgment becomes subjective. 'Objectivity' is a shaky word at the best of times. It could with some semblance of truth be used in times when artists and public agreed on a canon of perfection; then an artist could be measured on reaching or surpassing, or failing to reach, this standard of perfection, he could be seen to have been objectively good. We now live in a situation for which modern art historians have chosen the term 'non-normative aesthetics', taking the artist's work at his own evaluation and judging it as it exists, as a formal composition. It is this object which confronts us.

The means at the disposal of the artist are few – lines and colours making shapes and spaces. We read them as best we can. There are no set standards of achievement, therefore none of judgment. The formal solutions are novel in each case and have to be judged as success-ful within the frame of references set by the artist for the purpose. We are thus confronted with a game in which the rules as well as the scoring are arbitrary and if we think that we can take part in a game of which the rules can be varied at will, we are somewhat crazy if we expect to win. Therefore the spectator, too, has to make his own rules as he goes along and does his own scoring. These entirely non-Olympic games are known as art criticism, and the sooner we know that we are playing without rules, the better it will be. What is new in modern art is that the spectator – that is all of us – has been deliberately excluded from the world of the picture. We are not invited to walk in; we are told to stay out. The picture thus can only be observed from a distance, it is totally self-contained. We can see it, read it, but only with our mind. We have no other direct approach into the picture. Our expulsion from the understandable world of the picture is symptomatic of the separation of the artist from the spectator. The artist's social role has placed him in a world of his own, his activity is the making of the picture in complete freedom, free from social obligation, free from the public, entirely free to do what he wants – so runs the assumption.

'Freedom', said Picasso, 'one must be very careful with that. In painting as in everything else. Whatever you do you find yourself once more in chains. Freedom not to do one thing requires that you do another, imperatively. And there you have it, chains. That reminds me of a story of Jarry about the anarchist soldiers at drill. They are told: right face. And immediately, since they are anarchists, they all face left. . . . Painting is like that. You take freedom and you shut yourself up with your idea, just that particular one and no other. And there you are again, in chains.'[31] What we must learn to see is the higher responsi-bility disguised as irresponsibility, the higher discipline disguised as lack of discipline. We have to understand the artistic process not only as an attempted solution of a paradox, but as the paradox itself. What one knows, one cannot say, and once said, it is no more the same. Picasso was aware of it: '. . . If you take a spoken sentence and if you write it down exactly, with the same words, it becomes completely different and sometimes even to the contrary'.[32] What we have to understand is that no image is the image of something else, but only an image of itself alone, which in itself tries to encompass other forms of reality which have been active in the process of finding its own shape. Picasso never equated images with truth, in fact, it was Picasso who has made the most honest statement about art: 'Art is lies.'[33] That, of course, is the truth, or it would not be art. 'What truth?' said Picasso. 'Truth cannot exist. If I pursue a truth on my canvas, I can paint a hundred canvases with this same truth. Which one, then, is the truth? And what is truth – the thing that acts as my model, or what I am painting? Truth does not exist.'[34] Knowing this he explored every situation: 'I painted three canvases this afternoon,' he said. 'What's necessary is to do them, to do them, to do them! The more you paint, the nearer you get to something. That's the only way. . . . You must do as many as possible.'[35] Here lies the explanation for Picasso's urge to work in series, to work on and on, exploring one subject. His life's work is one long monologue, or better, dialogue with his pictures. Picasso was not only an artist who exemplified the complete unity of art and life, who is modern in the sense that the autonomy of his work is absolute, that he painted for no other reason than that he could not stop, because not to paint is not being a painter and that, to a painter, was not being alive. The problem is further complicated by the fact that he was so diabolically gifted, so much a natural painter that I could not imagine him not having been the greatest vase painter in Athens, or the man who would have painted the Sistine Chapel, if he had been around at the time.

Picasso was one of the strongest forces in the destruction of the Renaissance picture, in the abandonment of realism and illusion. As such he is considered one of the great modern artists. But if we look beyond the formal qualities of the picture, we shall find that Picasso is an astonishingly old-fashioned artist, a humanist concerned first with his picture as a formal achievement, but always with the condition of man, be it his own, or his models and friends, or man as such. Picasso had a wholly positive attitude to this world and this life and to all the things in it. In fact, he painted nothing but the joys and miseries of life, his own life most of all. All his work is autobiographical, of the very moment of creation. Picasso's work is the mirror of the world seen and experienced by him and him alone, and though it appears that he was a very wilful painter who forced his subjects into the shapes he intended, he was at the same time a very humble man who looked in silence at the world. 'One must, says Picasso, look for something that develops all by itself, something natural and not manufactured. Let it unfold as it is, "in the form of the natural and not in the form of 'art', the grass as grass, the tree as tree, the nude as nude". And so, down with everybody! Down with all that has been done! Down with Picasso, too!'[36] This is, philosophically, a strange position for the twentieth century, it is strictly platonic. Picasso hoped to paint the ideal, the essence. He felt and said that any form of art destroys the form of the natural (natural here not in the sense of appearance, but in the sense of essence), the tree as tree; 'Down with all that has been done', that is, down with all formal statements, including his own. He searched for a correspondence between the ideal and the actual; he knew that it does not exist and that he therefore could not ever find it, and yet he was driven to go on and on painting in the hope that each new work would be a nearer approximation to the truth he knew did not exist, or at least cannot be expressed in form. Hélène Parmelin asks: 'Then, is there nothing else but painting? Is it the major art? The only one perhaps that can truly re-create, on a terrible motionless plane, the reality beheld by the eye – but charged with intelligence – plus the reality of light and of the night and of our thoughts and of all that goes on around us? And yet, invent everything?'[37] And Picasso concluded: 'Make everything the same and everything something else.'[38] The artistic process is a process of metamorphosis, of changing forms of thought and awareness into other forms, none equivalent yet all expressive of some aspect of an outer and inner reality. The urge to find all the forms and relations is the driving power, but the process is inexhaustible and never ending. 'One always does the same thing, and yet one could do everything. What is there to stop us?'[39] The answer is the same thing is everything; art is one long process of finding pictorial equivalents for the artist's condition. When looking at his work, one has to recognise each one as a stage in his life, a new statement about a new Picasso in a new situation.

In Picasso's work we shall find very few formal portraits of himself, but he or his likeness appears in a thousand forms in his drawings and pictures. He enters in spirit and often in person every work he did, he is as ubiquitous in his paintings as it befits a creator. Plate 33 shows Pablo Picasso arriving in Paris in 1901, a self-portrait in the then latest fashion – a sporting artistic outfit – with mountaineering boots, ready to climb the heights of Paris, such as Montmartre and Montparnasse. He has already arrived at Montmartre as he stands outside the Moulin Rouge. He lived at the Bateau Lavoir with dozens of other outcasts. The days and nights of Montmartre suit his temperament and preference. The world of entertainment in the Paris around 1900 has not yet been seriously studied; not its history so much, but its significance. It is usually seen as the hectic market for erotic attractions, but it was a localised carnival not only of the senses but of the mind, and painters and poets flourish in the atmosphere not, as the philistine likes to think, because of the easygoing life, but on the contrary, for the discipline which freedom entails. I think that the identification of the artist with the cabaret and circus crowd, with the outcasts, is not accidental. It is not so much the gaiety of the scene, but the loneliness and the artificiality which makes the painter choose this identification. The severity of the discipline of the artiste is what the artists admired.

The monkey in *The Acrobat's Family with a Monkey*, 1905 (Plate 34)

Plate 33. Pablo Picasso: Self Portrait in front of the Moulin Rouge 1901
Ink and coloured pencil on paper 18 × 11·5 cm. *Private Collection*

was not to leave Picasso throughout his life; as a companion and as a
symbol, it was to come again and again into his work. In this picture it
seems to stand as the one excluded even from human·love. (The monkey
as painter had appeared in Goya's engraving, Plate 5.)

The conventional distinction between the 'portrait' and the 'model'
was changing. If there is a painting entitled 'Woman in a Green Hat',
and the painter or art historian identifies her as Mrs M, is it a portrait?
Even more awkward, when art historians identify the many nice girls
who served the artists as models for 'reclining nude', has the picture
become a portrait of Miss B? There is no binding answer, but it is worth
noting that the distinction has been lost. There is a change of role from
the sitter of the portrait to the model; the model is not any more the
model for a form, as in the life class, but becomes a person and as such
again becomes a portrait. We have thus found a dialectical jump.

Plate 34: Pablo Picasso: The Acrobat's Family with a Monkey 1905
Gouache, watercolour, pastel and indian ink on cardboard 104 × 75 cm.
Göteborgs Kunstmuseum, Göteborg

When the model sheds her artificiality of pretending to be Andromeda or the Seated Nude, Picasso makes an honest woman of her again by treating her not as a model, but as a living being. What Picasso paints is neither the object nor the subject. What he paints is not the thing or the person, what he paints is his relation to her. He paints what cannot be painted, and yet what fills the picture, his urge to possess and to understand. The painting is the meeting-point of that peculiar affair where the medium of paint becomes the love or the frustration, the failure or the fulfilment. One might say that the change of the role of the model is symptomatic of the emancipation of woman; she is no longer the servant, but the equal of the artist. Artist and model are now equal partners in the life of the picture. As an independent person the model is entitled to her own life, as her personal property. To the painter, however, the model or subject poses another question and that is his own role as an artist and the question of the function of his art. Thus this constantly recurring question becomes his autobiography; it is the artist and his model, that is, the artist and his own life. The approach to the model is at one and the same time the approach of a man to a woman, and of the artist to his work. The picture fights back, and the struggle in the subjection of the picture – which has its own laws and life – equates itself with the struggle with women, who also have their own laws and lives.

In modern art the completion of the painting is the battle between the laws of the picture and the will of the artist. The picture has become the battleground; in that sense all painting is action painting but the action is not one-sided. Plate 35 has a traditional title, *Nude in Red Armchair*. The statement is obviously true; it is also a nearly full-length portrait of Madame Marie-Thérèse Walter. If formerly the portrait was a public statement, it now becomes decidedly a private statement. The making of the picture is a game from which all seriousness should be banned. One can deduce from the picture that the game is the same and played with the same code of accident, luck, deception and resolution. What should be observed is simply that, in the game of transforming the girl into a picture, the forms make themselves independent and take part in the game: neither the girl nor the forms remain themselves, they enter a joint world where Picasso operates as a juggler with the re-assembled material which transforms itself all the time.

It is really a process of juggling with possibilities. The game is made less arbitrary by the fact that they are all controlled by an ordering principle, embodied by the artist; it is always controlled by the artist's intention and his aesthetic means. The process determines the result. The picture is no more a foregone conclusion, nor is it an accident, it is the synthesis of all the possibilities of the moment, and each moment has

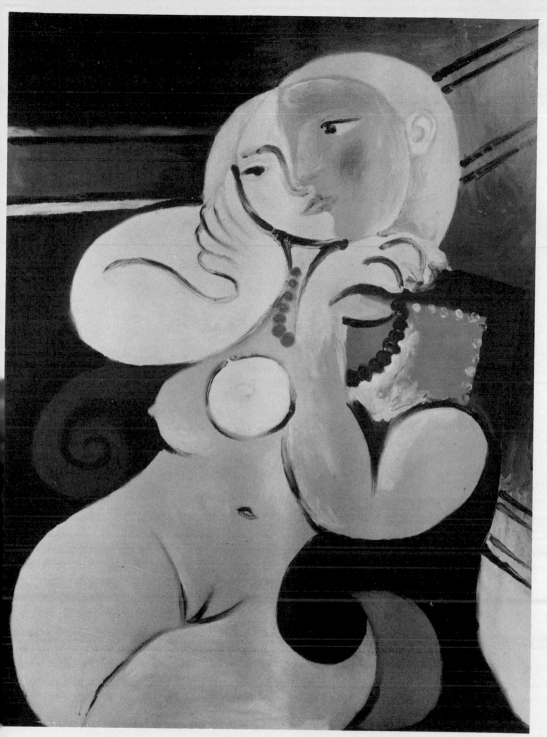

Plate 35. Pablo Picasso: Nude in Red Armchair 1932
Oil on canvas 129·8 × 95 cm. *Tate Gallery, London*

different possibilities. The 'double image' is the outcome of the Cubist experience and the inclusion of time and movement into the combined forms of experience: *Woman in a Fish Hat*, 19.4.1942 (Plate 36); the known woman turns into a myth. The person still previously herself in her many aspects and in the reflection of the many moods and possibilities of Picasso becomes his own statement with the figure as a dummy.

In the transformation of a woman into a picture, sometimes into a still life, all feelings have been formed into shapes, the shapes have aroused feelings. The elements of the picture have been constantly adjusted by the artist's actions, and the artist's actions by the picture. What remains at the end is the artist's activity on his material. That is the situation of the artist in his search for his truth and its equivalent in the form of form, and the knowledge that his quest is in vain. Truly a Don Quixote. He leaves behind on his forlorn pilgrimage the works of art which accumulate as the remnants of his despair. In a sense they are all failures and they are also his victories in the battle with the picture. In the process of work, Picasso creates his identity as a painter as he questions the relation of himself to his subject. From the many thousands of drawings and paintings of the subject 'Artist and Model', his preoccupation with this theme can be judged, it is really the problem of 'art' and the process of artistic activity. He is in his pictures always the painter painting. He paints the process of work. His art defines itself in that unity of theory and praxis.

Picasso's work is an autobiography, but as he was both inside and outside his pictures, he appears very frequently in the picture in a visible form, as a likeness or just as often in disguise, as a man, as a faun, as a clown, as a satyr. He can choose the woman and as a painter can invent her shapes to suit himself. But as happy and light-hearted as the pictures may be, underneath there lies a very old human tragedy, that of the failing powers of creation and the knowledge of an end to self-consciousness. Picasso was never concerned with death – he was not a Christian artist – he was concerned with life, but he knew that it would last only as long as his powers lasted. Life for Picasso was essentially a full, long, pagan rite.

Already in 1901 *Nude* with Picasso at her feet (Plate 37) is not just a love scene; it is the artist looking at his model with the eyes of the painter, but also with the eyes of a man. Picasso, later in life, makes the theme 'Artist and Model', 'Man and Woman' the subject of most of his work. He restates his case as a painter and as a man. His symbolic language needs images and he disguises himself as the principle of virility. Like the Greek gods, he can take any form to impress woman, and he chooses the most tried and effective models. In this Protean endeavour to take new forms, however, he acts as the clown who knows

Plate 36. Pablo Picasso: Woman in a Fish Hat 1942
Oil on canvas 98·1 × 81·4 cm. *Stedelijk Museum, Amsterdam*

the difference between the persona and the mask. Picasso disguised is
still Picasso laughing behind the mask. As an artist he fools the figures
in the picture, not himself and not wholly the spectator; the game is
played with the mask lifted. *Artist as Clown and Model*, 1953 (Plate 38);
Nude with Monkey Painting, 1954 (Plate 39); here the lascivious
monkey has again taken the part of the painter. The pictures from a
long series, all of the same month, January 1954, make the game
perfectly clear: *Nude with Masked Cupid* (Plate 40). The artist's work is
the day to day reaction to himself, to his work personified by the model
transformed into a painting, and all the time that he is acting upon and
reacting against his material he recreates his identity as a painter, and all
the time that he paints, he is aware of the problem of being a painter.

Plate 37. Pablo Picasso: Nude
(with Picasso at her
Feet) 1901
Ink and watercolour on
paper 17·6 × 23·2 cm.
*Museo Picasso,
Barcelona*

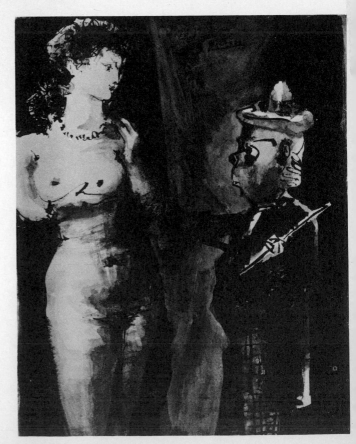

Plate 38. Pablo Picasso: Artist as
Clown and Model 1953
Brush drawing and
watercolour. *Verve,
Vol. 8, No. 29–30*

Plate 39. Pablo Picasso: Nude with Monkey Painting 1954 Brush drawing. *Verve*, *Vol*. 8, *No*. 29–30

Plate 40. Pablo Picasso: Nude with Masked Cupid 1954 Brush drawing. *Verve*, *Vol*. 8, *No*. 29–30

Plate 41. Pablo Picasso: Artist and Model March–May, 1963
Oil on canvas 129·8 × 162·3 cm. *Private Collection*

He thought and acted not only the role of the artist, but he raised the
question of the relation of the artist to his surroundings.

And still later in life, in 1963, Picasso painted a new series of artist and
model, but here the artist is the main figure; the concern is always with
the meaning of painting: (Plates 41 and 42). The problem remains always
the same, only the solutions are different. *Picture in Studio: Artist Painting*, 22.2.1963 (Plate 43) summarises the idea of the artist as artist, sur-
rounded by the works of art he has made from living models, making
more pictures from models he has made, metamorphosing life into art,

Plate 42. Pablo Picasso: Artist and Model June, 1963
Oil on canvas 92 × 60 cm. *Private Collection*

art into life, and going on endlessly because there is no end. This paint-ing, with its medieval atmosphere, its traces of sorcery, the smell of the transmutation of metals, reminds one of the study of Dr Faustus. We are looking into the alchemist's workshop, in his search for the philosopher's stone, which will transmute life into art. He knows it cannot be done, that is his curse, and that he must go on doing it, that is his salvation.

Plate 43: Pablo Picasso: Picture in Studio: Artist Painting, February, 1963
Oil on canvas 95·8 × 129·8 cm. *Private Collection*

4

Emotion and Expression

The individual response of an artist to his situation can take different forms. One and the same idea can find entirely different forms of expression in the picture, and very similar pictorial motives can contain entirely different ideas. Several important concerns of the modern artists are: the return to Primitivism; the role of woman; the artist and the model; the question of the artist's identity. All have been the concern of Picasso, but how simple and unquestioning were his solutions. How torturing and questioning those of the Expressionists are, we shall have to discuss. Picasso solved his problems in his life and in his pictures; the tortured artist solves the problems in his soul. Picasso dealt with the problem of the artist as a man and as a working man. His question is that of the artist at work – painting – his models, himself, his working life. But the existential painter is not concerned with his life as lived: he does not paint man, but the destiny of man; not woman, but the destiny of woman. The difficulty of man is that he is still a somewhat irrational being, living in a rational world. The problem has been defined the other way round: that man is a rational being living in an irrational world. But I do not accept this. There is nothing wrong with the world, until man upsets it. A series of well ascertainable facts should give him confidence and enhance his reason, yet he worries about his place in the world, his destiny, as he calls it.

Kierkegaard brought 'eternity' back into 'time', as Löwith says. He made the individual afraid of being in the world.[40] Three years after the Communist Manifesto, Kierkegaard recommends 'the testing of one's self' and complains that people believe in the spirit of the time or even the spirit of the world, but not in the Holy Ghost.[41] The German word *Geist* means 'ghost' as well as 'spirit', and the spiritual (das Geistige) begins to haunt the artists' thoughts. We are hence dealing with ghosts and we have found one motive of Expressionism, because it deals with ghosts. The problem of existence is the problem of the unique individual in the paintings of lost souls. In the ideas of Kierkegaard a key can be found to the understanding of Expressionism. It is the art of man in despair. Though he is unique, he does not believe in the humanity of man; in fact, the existential position is anti-humanist and degrades man who is in existential ideology his sole concern. Expressionism exalts man in his unique position and in that final subjectivity of romanticism destroys him. His undoing is not his collective reason, but his self-inflicted unreason; in search of his destiny he looses his world and himself.

We encounter in Expressionism the ghosts of man, the shadows of his existential nothingness. The pathetic pilgrimage of ghosts begins with Ensor and Munch, the existential painters of Angst, as afraid of death as of life, of man as of woman. The underlying theme of all Expressionist art is cultural despair, despair with the culture of one's own day, which matured in the climate of Kierkegaard and Nietzsche, Dostoievsky and Strindberg. This cultural despair sought the solution of the ills of our culture in a return to the sources, the origins, the childhood of mankind, when a state of bliss and innocence, virile youthful strength was supposed to have animated mankind.

In the nineteenth century vast numbers of shady theories were formulated on vague assumptions: the theory of young nations overcoming old nations, a justification for imperialism (as in Germany), a revival of old folk customs, an adulation of youth, a return to the simple ways of the peasant; altogether a revolt against the industrial city, against modernity, against liberalism, capitalism and progress. This becomes a political question; the world has seen or learned some of the ghastly results, but rarely considered the artistic expression of the situation. The lesson to be drawn is that much of modern art, though it looked new, was in fact not modern at all – in intention – but reactionary art in modern guise, directed against modern civilisation and against the intellect, appealing to emotion, folk memory and primitivism of heart and mind.

The return to primitivism in aesthetics which, as a stylistic feature of modern art, is one thing, but a wholly different motivation gave rise to a return to folk and primitive culture in the Expressionist world, leading by necessity to entirely different formal uses of the ideas. Primitivism in art at the beginning of the twentieth century had two different aims, though the outward appearance may be misleading. Picasso used the formal structural qualities of Negro art to enrich his knowledge of formal possibilities. The Expressionists, on the other hand, used the forms as an emotional statement of identification with primitive forces. For Picasso, the ideology of primitivism did not exist, only the formal qualities to be exploited as a valid vocabulary of formal language. To the redemptionists of the Expressionist tendency, the ideology of purity and simplicity fitted in with the native, folkish, earthbound prejudices. How can the naked individual soul find its own salvation? This is the fundamental question of the Expressionist artist and it is solved in accordance with the fundamentalist attitude of the Protestant sects.

It was a moral intention which led the Expressionists to a search for the lost purity of art, a return to the 'primitive' virtue, that is, to the simple, innocent, fundamentalist concept of pure virgin art, to be found in the childhood of man. This is the exact parallel to the fundamentalist attitude in the religious revivals of the nineteenth century, a revolt against book learning, a revolt against the antique, the classical, the ordered disciplines of thought. The self-taught, impassioned and inspired teacher stated his claims against the school-trained, reasoning cleric. The whole history of the Evangelists from Wesley to Moody and Sankey lies outside our field, but not its spiritual aims and intentions, because it points to the fact that Expressionism is essentially a manifestation of the fundamentalist dilemma. Expressionism shares with fundamentalism anti-romanism and anti-classicism. The classical language of form, that is Greco-Roman Renaissance language, had been valid until the nineteenth century.

This is essentially correct, even for Germany and the countries on the fringes of the Roman Empire, but it is equally correct to note that this language was never as firmly rooted there or as well spoken as in the classic arena. The French painters, when deforming the classical language, had to depart from the norm. The German painters had neither the normative tendency nor the same easy control. They never possessed that grasp of form which is the distinguishing mark of classic art. The difference of form was already marked in the work of Cranach and Grünewald; there a greater individuality and a more self-willed expression was prevalent.

Each Expressionist painting is the effusion of the moment, the direct and unfettered expression of a personal urge, an uncontrolled, spontaneous outburst, created in frenzy. It could not search for form, only for content, and the content, be it expressed as a landscape, a still life or a religious subject, is placed and not composed. That a picture still demands arrangement goes without saying, but that is a necessity with which the spontaneous act of painting has to come to terms. Not all Expressionist paintings live up to that spontaneity and quite a few are almost traditionally well-composed pictures of townscapes or portraits, but the intention is the direct fixation of an emotional inner state of awareness.

Expressionism is by definition the immediate projection of the state of the soul, and no picture was ever intended to be 'of something' other than the artist's spontaneous, uncensored outburst. As Cassou states: '. . . a lack of true plastic tradition, a want of skill in seizing semblances and giving them dignity of form, a fundamental impossibility to obtain from such exercises the same satisfaction as the Latins who bring to them the full severity of their taste and culture, and, on the other hand, a desperate need of unreality, or rather of a moral explanation of reality.'[42] Northern art tends to deal with the human condition much more than with the condition of objects. The relation of man to man, man to God, are its main concerns, and the relation of man to nature is treated not as a visual encounter but as a mystic union. Thus it is that youth, redemption, death, desire, the strong father, the fallen king, the vile woman, the monster, the forest, the sea, the night, are the images which haunt the Expressionists. This state of the soul, due to the Protestant concern with individual guilt and the loneliness of the soul in this world, makes the artist suffer from the same agonising inability to retain their emotions in form.

Territorially, Expressionism is a feature of the borderlands of the Catholic universe, those parts where reform, revolt and dissent spread and was either violently suppressed or victorious, the Hussites in Prague, the Anabaptists at Münster. It is another way of saying that the classical tradition in thought as well as in form grew weaker towards the periphery, and that those outlying parts of the Roman, later the Roman Catholic, Empire were on the borderlines of the metropolitan civilisation. The territory of modern Expressionism is Belgium and Holland, Scandinavia, Bohemia, Saxony, Westphalia, the German Marches and the twilight countries between separate cultures.

The stylistic models which the Expressionists searched for were Bavarian glass paintings of peasant simplicity and, more revealing, the late medieval woodcuts which contained not only the simple forms but also the millennial feelings of the movement arising after the Black Death, the Apocalypses and Dances of Death and the agonies of Grünewald – these became the inspirations for their work. The Dance of Death, in the late Middle Ages the symbol of equality (in death all: bishops and beggars, statesmen and thieves are equal), was at the time an egalitarian statement of the revolt of the poor expressed in Christian imagery. The Dance of Death of the Expressionists poses the existential dilemma in a new guise, or disguise, in the form of the mask. The dance of skeletons and masks in the works of Ensor is related to the more robust Dance of Death of Rouault. The mask, that shield of a hidden identity, becomes the equivalent of the Christian invisible soul which has nowhere to go.

The mask is a recurring motif in modern art. It appears in two entirely separate forms, both pointing to different responses to the artist's own persona and situation. With Picasso, it can be read as part of the game of deception; the mask itself is an artefact which hides the evil or benign designs of the artist. Picasso is using the mask as part of his comedy. The other use of the mask is that of tragedy, particularly the tragedy of the artist's identity. It is used in that sense by the Expressionists. There the tragic question 'Who am I?', already asked by Gauguin, raises the problem of existence and identity, to which there is no verdict because there is no judge, unless one intends to be jury, judge and accused in one. But that exactly is their problem; they are the self-accused who carry the guilt of their own accusation. They live in a prison of their own making, they are their own jailers and their own inmates. In their work it is not just the occasional use of a tragic mask, but, much more worrying, the mask as the face, the face frozen as a mask. There is a terrified rigidity in the hideous grimace and the pain distorted imagery of mask-like faces. Whoever they are – prostitutes, dancers, women, men, the artist himself – all are doomed. The real problem to them is not death, as in Christian imagery, but life. The ages of man from birth to death is a favourite theme, but the central problem is the life they cannot live.

The formal expression of man's search for his own identity is confused by social guilt which man has created for himself by his attitude to his own counterpart in the actual world, that is, to woman. For an understanding of some important aspects of modern art one has to consider the new role of women in social life and with it that of woman in art. The new relation of artist and model as expressed by Picasso was a real human relation. The Expressionists have quite different problems. An answer has to be found by descending from the great moral abstractions into the lower regions of actual social life. The question formulates itself with Art Nouveau and the heyday of bourgeois expansion in Paris and London, Berlin and Vienna, accompanied by the prophets of redemption who nevertheless are entangled in the network of social relations. The dilemma of good intentions without the means of accomplishing them robs the artist of his strength, and he almost parades his weakness as a redeeming fable.

But the paradox goes further: the feebleness of the artist was really an inversion of the actual state of society, because the world they lived in was one of male domination, the last period of masculine assertion as represented by the Victorian father, the French male-dominated family and the German barracks' attitude to women. Power was vested in man. The heroine of Art Nouveau is Woman, the Woman that never was. The ideal, too good for this world, was endowed with all the virtues, representing as a nude statue all the virtues of capitalism, with a wheel she represents industry, with a raised arm education, with a torch freedom, with outstretched arms, love, and so we find idealised woman on pedestals standing in for the missing virtues. Marx saw it clearly in his polemic with a then and still unimportant Protestant pastor. He writes: 'Herr Daumer naturally does not say a word about the present situation of women – on the contrary, it is a question only of the female as such.

He tries to console women for their social distress, by making them the object of a . . . cult.'[43] The bourgeois manufacturers saw the point: those ideal maidens did not resemble their mill girls at all. They were then at liberty to sacrifice on the altar of pure womanhood, and to feel no guilt about the real women who bore no resemblance to the ideal.

But the thing becomes even more absurd because the period also produced the highest forms of visual pornography. Thus we find in the period two totally opposed images of woman united by their opposition: the virgin and the prostitute. Such considerations are, or should be, part of art history as they are the structure of pictorial imagery. In Art Nouveau as well as in Expressionism, the artists were obsessed by the idea of Woman as the unobtainable dream, as the goddess on the pedestal. In that form she appears in art in complete inversion to her social existence. The very idealising of Art Nouveau reveals itself as the shame-faced disguise of sexual emancipation. In fact, as the ideological cloak for the actual social process which drove women into factories and offices and eventually made them almost equal wage-earners. This actual process could not, of course, be faced in actual terms, that is not the artist's role in society. His aim is to disguise.

Pictorial art casts a thin screen over social reality and obscures its true relations, but it also disguises the morals which arise within the social reality, and these are compounded of male arrogance, exploitation and domination of man over women. The analysis then reads like this: the christian conscience equated sin with lust; the female of the cult is supposed to be free from both and yet leads men into the ways of sin, a paradox which did not puzzle bourgeois thinkers. This fiction was tenable when women had no rights and they were, so to say, taking vengeance on man, but once they were becoming independent, man had to share some of the guilt which he so cheerfully had reserved for women. In Art Nouveau, the woman is presented as the incarnation of sin (Beardsley, Stuck) and man as the victim. It is men's revenge on woman's emancipation, yet the whole fabrication is transferred into a purely decorative and non-existent world. In Art Nouveau, woman becomes the fallen idol of bourgeois society, yet she dominates the scene in a way which points to her actual rise in social life. The preoccupation with sin is a remnant of the Christian hangover, the preoccupation with ideal woman a bourgeois illusion and the equivalent of the socially useless woman which was the bourgeois ideal. The role which 'woman' plays in Art Nouveau and Expressionism is the inversion of her own allegory.

We then reach the next stage of the paradox; woman in social life approaching equality. Pre-Raphaelite women lived in the decorative never-never land of allegory. Here, too, live Hodler's women, but these

very same pure creatures allegorising sin as well as virtue become in the
Expressionist movement carnal women. The prostitute as the victim of
man becomes the theme; not the happy, business-like brothel of
Toulouse-Lautrec, whose social realism never obscures the economics
of supply and demand, but the tortured woman racked by doubts.

It was at that time that pseudo-philosophers invented the battle of
the sexes. To read the graphic works of Munch correctly, one has to
read them as intending to give form to that battle of the sexes where
man and woman struggle for supremacy; the sexual battle is only the
disguise for the social struggle. In the German-speaking world the
revolt against bourgeois values had taken on a new form and a new
ideological disguise; it was described as the battle of the generations.
In English 'Sons and Fathers' and the ills of the social order were
ascribed to the older generation; it was they who had created the false
values from which the young were to be free, thus shifting the social
problem to a sexual plane and annihilating it in the process of shifting
the ground.

The ideological inversions find their equivalent expressions in the
picture. It would be wrong to consider Munch as a 'Symbolist' because
in his work the recurring symbols of the Cry, the Sea, Death, as the
expression of loneliness and despair, are not so much symbols as
experiences. Munch's existence was shaped in symbolic forms and his
pictures are the statements of his real state of being. It would in any
case be wrong to assume that an Expressionist ever paints anything
outside himself. *Evening in Karl-Johan Street*, 1892 (Plate 44): a procession of ghosts disguised as people, or a procession of people disguised as ghosts, the illuminated houses are not the abodes of the
living, the street is really a Styx leading to the underworld, and the tree
is doom-shaped, a word invented by Thurber who is somewhat in-
debted to Munch, though he turned the battle of the sexes into a parlour
game. *The Chamber of Death* of *c*. 1892 (Plate 45) is also an existential
painting; the isolation of each figure in space, the isolation of the dying,
all the loving care and concern of the family expressed in the action, is
negated by the placing of the figures. Each one is alone in his grief, each
man dies for himself alone, and every death leaves the individual sur-
vivor lonelier still. Death does not unite, death separates not only the
dead from the living, but the living from each other. Another work is
called *Anxiety* of 1894 (Plate 46); Angst – the very word of existential-
ism from Kierkegaard to Sartre – the procession over the bridge into
the unknown, high above the harbour and the town, where real life, the
life of trade and activity, takes place. Man is here suspended between a
poisoned heaven and a receding world on his way to his unknown
destiny.

Plate 44. Edvard Munch: Evening in Karl-Johan Street in Oslo 1892
Oil on canvas 84·5 × 121 cm. *Munch-Museet, Oslo*

Madonna, a coloured lithograph of 1895 (Plate 47): a strange
Madonna, nearer to Stuck's *Sin*, the halo in red, really the colour of the
devil's whore in Christian mythology, the snakes of Medusa, the face
of a seductress, and with all that a sacred intention. The ambiguity of
the role of woman is here symbolised to perfection; the idol, the saint,
the temptress – sin and sacrifice. The Three Stages of Woman – Know-
lcdgc, Lust, Innocence – are really too literal to carry the conviction
Munch intended (Plate 48). The image of lust corresponds to the proto-
type of the period, *The Medusa* by Aubrey Beardsley and Stuck's *Sin*.
The symbolism of the colour is all too obvious: white for innocence,
blue-black for sadness or fidelity, and red for love and life. On the
bridge or by the sea Munch poses the problem of life: where are his
figures going? the black sea calls to suicide or birth; woman is forced

Plate 45. Edvard Munch: The Chamber of Death c.1892
Oil on canvas 150 × 167·5 cm. *National Gallery, Oslo*

by her destiny; there are two roads, one upwards, the future, one down into oblivion, and it appears as if the choices were unimportant.

In the work of Rouault, too, the world presents its problem in the form of masks, of dummies of the Guignol. Man is imprisoned or he plays a part in a play which he does not understand. *The Three Judges*, 1913 (Plate 49) with farcical masks. *Circus Girl, c.* 1925–30 (Plate 50); here the mask corresponds more to reality where in actual life a mask is also adopted. *Woman Regarding herself in a Mirror*, 1906 (Plate 51), a recurring topos of identity. The problems of Nolde and Rouault are closely related, except that Rouault in the classical tradition tries to reassemble them like stained glass, while Nolde, quite outside the formalism of the classical language, struggles for the forms of his expression. *Pentecost*, 1909 (Plate 52); *The Life of Christ* (centre panel: Crucifixion), 1911–12 (Plate 53).

77

Plate 46. Edvard Munch: Anxiety 1894
Oil on canvas 94 × 74 cm. *Munch-Museet, Oslo*

Plate 48. Edvard Munch: Woman (The Sphinx) 1899
Lithograph 46·2 × 59·2 cm. *Kornfeld and Klipstein, Berne*

Plate 47. Edvard Munch:
Madonna – Loving
Woman 1895
Lithograph 60·5 × 44·2
cm. *Kornfeld and
Klipstein, Berne*

Plate 49. Georges Rouault: The Three Judges 1913
      Gouache and oil on cardboard 76·4 × 104·1 cm. *Museum of Modern Art,
New York, Sam A. Lewisohn Bequest*

Plate 50. Georges Rouault: The Circus Girl *c.*1925–30
Oil on paper on canvas 64·3 × 45·3 cm. *Glasgow Museum and Art Gallery*

Plate 51. Georges Rouault: Woman Regarding herself in a Mirror 1906
Watercolour on cardboard 70 × 53 cm. *Musée National d'Art Moderne,
Paris*

Plate 52. Emil Nolde: Pentecost 1909
Oil on canvas 87 × 107 cm. *Emil Nolde Foundation, Seebüll*

Plate 53. Emil Nolde: The Life of Christ (centre panel): Crucifixion 1911–12
Oil on canvas 220 × 191 cm. *Emil Nolde Foundation, Seebüll*

James Ensor *The Entry of Christ into Brussels* (detail, Plate 54). In this painting the millennial hopes as well as the irony of a Christ coming into the modern world are fused. A carnival procession of masks, such is the existential position in which artists like Munch and

Plate 54. James Ensor: The Entry of Christ into Brussels (detail) 1888
Oil on canvas 250 × 434 cm. overall *Collection Col. Louis Franck, London,
on loan to the Royal Museum of Fine Arts, Antwerp*

85

Ensor find themselves; it is the mental climate in which Expressionism becomes understandable as a necessity.

　　While Nolde, Ensor and Rouault are struggling with a Christian imagery and a search for expression of the human condition in Christian terms or symbols, other artists are transferring the problem into the contemporary world, and ask the unanswerable question. Man and woman are lost in a modern setting, they face each other in silence, they stare into mirrors, they become the slaves of the wind or of music, as in Kokoschka's *Windsbraut* (*The Bride of the Wind*), 1914 (Plate 55). The many Expressionist paintings of woman looking in a mirror may pose the question of woman's identity, or show a concern with her appearance, but in either case it is the question of the persona; who am I? how do I appear to others? The same question is raised in the masquerade picture by Beckmann of 1925, *The Artist with his Wife* going to the Carnival (Plate 56); a public presentation becomes a private

Plate 55. Oskar Kokoschka: The Bride of the Wind 1914
Oil on canvas 181 × 221 cm. *Kunstmuseum, Basle*

Plate 56. Max Beckmann: The Artist with his Wife 1925
Oil on canvas 160 × 104 cm. *Kunstmuseum, Düsseldorf*

disguise or, more likely, a private revelation of the artist as dummy or clown in the image of the marionette man himself, asserting his privacy behind a mask. Women do not seem to need a mask – they can use their natural body or their artificial hats to change their image of identity at will. Kirchner in his *Half Length Nude with Hat* (Plate 57) makes a picture of a woman presenting her riddle to the eyes of men.

Plate 57. Ernst Ludwig Kirchner: Half Length Nude with Hat 1911
Oil on canvas 76 × 70 cm. *Wallraf-Richartz Museum, Cologne*

In the drawing for his play 'Murder, Hope of Women' by Kokoschka (Plate 58), the confrontation in the battle of the sexes becomes final. The theme and the imagery are all equivalents for the state of man and his fear of existence. In a religious or a non-religious guise the problem remains; man faces society as an inexplicable riddle in a total denial of rationality and knowledge; fear stalks the world in the cloak of the riddle of existence.

Plate 58. Oskar Kokoschka: Murder, Hope of Women c.1908
Pen and ink 21·5 × 17·4 cm. *Staatsgalerie, Stuttgart*

5

The Naïve Vision

In this chapter we shall be concerned with two related but in themselves strictly contradictory questions, the primitive and the naïve. The important difference is that one is an artistic problem, the primitive, and the other is a strictly non-artistic problem, the naïve. The word 'naïve' has been used since the eighteenth century as part of the intellectual heritage of Jean-Jacques Rousseau. The French 'naïf' comes from the Latin word 'nativus', meaning natural, original, as from birth. During the eighteenth century the term naïf was used in the battle against the courtly art of the Rococo, that playful, precious, over-sophisticated style. The word naïf stood for the unsophisticated, non-artificial, innocent, unspoilt, natural. 'Schiller in 1795 defined the concept of the "naïve" as opposed to the "sentimentalische" (sentimental). . . . The naïve person . . . experiences naturally; the sentimental person "experiences nature" (das Natürliche) as a lost paradise, as a desirable state of being."[44]

A great reversal of taste began when the Romantics sought out the Primitives, which led a hundred years later to the enthusiasm for Negro sculpture. This owed much of its impetus to a reaction against classical doctrine. To realise the magnitude of the impact of primitive art on the painters of the twentieth century, it must be remembered that the canon of beauty, or the aesthetics, of the European tradition had an uninterrupted language of forms based on the classical Greek ideal. In fact, the language of forms had a longer tradition than the unity of the space concept. The Greek ideal was lost with the decline of the Roman Empire and revived in the Renaissance, but even through the Christian art of the Middle Ages in its Byzantine, Romanesque and Gothic forms, it was never far away and traces of it remained (far from the ideal, but near enough) in the language of forms. To break down this European aesthetic, which looked eternal, was one of the stylistic revolutions of the years around 1900. Treating style as formal organisation instead of something much more important and relevant than that which appears on the surface of a painting is not sufficient. Primitivism, a return to the days when the world was a better place and art must have existed in a purer form, more original and innocent, original in the sense of nearer the origin of mankind, is a Utopian idea.

The idea that things were better in the past is an old story. The Golden

Age lives on, though it has often been exploded. 'Marx did not believe in the possibility of a return to naïve immediacy of natural existence, which it is not certain ever existed, as the Romantics assumed, much even to Hegel's scorn. Lenin criticised it too: "That primitive man obtained all he required as a free gift of nature is a silly fable. . . . There has never existed a Golden Age, and primitive man was absolutely crushed by the burden of existence, by the difficulties of the struggle against nature." '[45] (From, appropriately, *The Agrarian Question and the 'Critics of Marx'*.)[46]

This seeking for the primitive arose in painters as one manifestation of the general belief that in all fields of human endeavour things had been getting worse, not better; the artists shared the belief that a golden age of innocence had once existed which had been destroyed by industrial-isation and urbanisation. It was a nostalgia bordering on despair. In the world of art the rediscovery of the Primitives, meaning pre-Renaissance painters, Giotto and Cimabue, led to the first definition given to this aim. The idea that art has a life-cycle – youth–maturity–decay – corresponded to simple-minded sciences such as Vitalism, hence the idea of decline, decay, old age, sterility. Any revival must be a rejuvenation: back to the origins of Art was the battle cry. It is quite logical that the forms of art will correspond to the aim.

The distinction has to be made between the varying lessons which different artists drew from that common source of Primitive Art.[47] To painters like Gauguin and, later, the German Expressionists, only the sentimental, exotic and in their view simple and primitive life and its motives appealed. To Picasso and some other painters the very forms and structures of Primitive Art became meaningful. It is for that reason that the explosive potential of primitive form, when built into the picture, proved much more destructive and therefore constructive, than the idealising motives of the modern Romantics. What came as a shock to the public was the appearance of savage forms, of frightening exotic masks and carvings. Their strength and terrible beauty was discovered by Derain, Vlaminck, Picasso and others in Paris. But what had preceded this discovery was the beginning of a shift from the eurocentric viewpoint. The old belief that savage tribes were naturally inferior and that the revealed religion of Christ was as naturally superior as capitalism was to cannibalism was slowly being undermined. Genuine ethnography and anthropology, historical studies of comparative religion, a new approach to the historic development of society had recognised progress and advance and also established the relative validity of different cultures in their social time and space. In brief, the firmly held belief that good could only come out of Rome or Manchester was being shaken.

The introduction of primitive forms into Western art was an implicit recognition of the equal validity of all forms of human expression. To the artists the problem must have presented itself in a much more simple and direct form. They saw what they needed and they took what they had seen. Their action was made possible by the new readiness to accept a multitude of standards in ethics and aesthetics. The painters simply saw some forms they had hoped for and immediately used them, but once employed in the picture these forms developed their own life and demands and transformed the whole picture. Gauguin's visits to what he believed to be primitive and happy people was less significant than the appearance of those far from happy primitive forms in the picture itself. The forms of a pictorial language not only carry a meaning, but are in themselves meaningful. In art, as Frankl has said, 'forms become the symbol of meaning'.[48]

The truth that form and content are one is still known outside Europe. A visiting student from Africa asked if it were true that Europeans collect African masks for the decoration of their living-rooms. When told that it was true, he shuddered and said 'Don't they know that they contain medicine?' This story suggests that with the forms some of the spirit had also entered Western aesthetics, and without pursuing the argument of the efficacy of magic it appears that forms as symbols contain in their shapes more than just their shapes, or that their choice and acceptance tells us something about ourselves. To quote Burckhardt, 'We shall never get rid of the Greeks until we become Barbarians ourselves.'[49]

There is a difference, however, between the deliberate use of these forms by very sophisticated artists and a related but very different phenomenon, that of the naïve vision of the untaught painter. The breakdown in the aesthetics of the West made the acceptance of the naïve painter possible, and it was not an accident that they were discovered by the sophisticated artists in search of the primitive. It is also not accidental that at the beginning of the century the art of children was being accepted and eventually cultivated. What was happening was the discovery of the primitive in one's own backyard.

We now have to turn to the tragi-comedy of the naïve painters, because they were selected for the very reasons which they themselves would have rejected; they became the victims of a cruel joke which they could not understand. They were taken seriously for the – to them – wrong reasons. That is why it is not their work but the acceptance of their work which is of contemporary relevance. The naïve is by definition non-art, which is one of the secrets why it was accepted. All the Naïve painters – using the term 'naïve' rather than the more frequently used but misleading term 'Primitive' – Rousseau, Séraphine, Vivin,

Bombois, Csontvary, all painted for the wrong reasons and were discovered for the right ones. That, of course, is an unkind statement and
can only be understood within the class structure of our society and its
art. All the Naïve painters were working-class or petty bourgeois and
uneducated. They painted the way they did because they knew no better
and it was their betters who decided that they were on to something,
on to which the painters themselves were not. The whole thing was a
cruel joke perpetrated by the upper class of artists and critics on the
unsuspecting naïve and honest working man and woman.

The discovery of the Naïve was a sort of slumming of the sophisticated. But it was serious and significant; the educated artists were searching for new, unspoilt, unused forms of expression which they sought in a
return to the forms of the primitive, in the true sense, in savage carvings,
in medieval folk art, outside their own time and culture, until they
discovered that in their own time and town there were primitive relics,
untutored and unspoilt children, if not of nature, then of the slums, who
had escaped the sterile knowledge of the academies and who, like
children, developed their own language of forms. The cruel paradox,
however, was that the Naïve painters were striving for the very accom-
plishments, including the recognition and dignity of the Academy and,
like all amateurs, they failed to see the shortcomings in their own work
measured by the standards of their own ideal. The one peremptory
statement is that none of the Naïve painters wanted to be naïve, and
none knew that he was. It was their superiors in skill and knowledge
who admired them for the very shortcomings which, had they but known
them, would have caused the poor to despair. Unaware of their failings,
they were also unaware of their strength, because the two are identical.
It was because of their failings that they had to force the strength of
their vision into awkward, unskilled, unused forms, and in these forms
their intentions came to life, different from what they had hoped or
ever knew.

The way had been paved for the acceptance of the honest intention
which lacked the accomplished skill of the professional by the work of
Van Gogh, a painter without a facile talent, so much so that the fire of
his intention had to burn through his inability to express himself. In
that fire his very weakness was consumed and replaced by a strength
not seen before. Sheer will-power and not talent is the force of his work
and it remains all the greater for it, but that is exactly a modern discern-
ment to take the seriousness more seriously than the polish of mechanical
accomplishment. It had taken the best part of the nineteenth century
to do away with the concept that the making of art is a skill reserved
for members of academies. The Naïve painters still believed it, because
they aimed at the polished picture and nothing is more revealing than

the self-conscious 'finish' of a Douanier Rousseau. The modern artists and critics were up to date: the Naïve painters were not.

No offence is intended by including in this field some painters who are rightly recognised as great artists, such as Van Gogh and Chagall. Their acceptance as great artists is based on our recognition of the naïve as a powerful form of expression. It is exactly the immediacy, what used to be called the violence, of Van Gogh which disturbed his contemporaries, and what impresses us as the directness of his statement. We have long learned not to judge a picture by its skill or 'finish', as it was called, the faultless rendering of things seen. We have come to accept as a historic process a revision of prejudices and a change in our expectation. What staggers us is the clumsy honesty of that unsophisticated vision which for its lack of subtlety, even for its lack of knowledge of such subtlety, impresses us directly with its childish logic. It embarasses us with its bluntness like the occasional wisdom dropping from the mouth of an illiterate peasant and for a brief moment we can believe that truth comes from the lips of fools and children and that innocence and ignorance are a blessing. Such are the reasons for the new acceptance and respectability of the Naïve vision which had always existed, at least as long as society has been divided into separate classes of knowledge and education. Before that historic state we have primitive art with its own high sophistication shared by all members of the community; thereafter we have the naïve, which is only possible if the largest section of the population is left out of the higher culture. It is in the layers of the subcultures that the naïve is found.

Has it or has it not a genuine claim to be considered in its own right as art at all?'There is one criterion which does make the Naïve vision completely convincing. It is difficult to describe, yet easy to understand, and it is of relevance in the whole field of art. There is no English word for what French artists call 'réalisé' which does not mean 'realised', but it means something like 'thereness'. If an object or a scene is not just painted, no matter how well, but if it is decidedly *there*, a French painter will say 'ça c'est réalisé'. In English perhaps the word 'presence' is the best. If a thing has a presence, like an actor who fills the stage without saying a word or doing anything, that sort of presence is what the term describes. Once one looks for it, one knows it; most pictures by Picasso are *there*, a Van Gogh is *there*, but not every Renoir is *there*. In that sense, most Primitives are *there*, often too much so, but there is no doubt about their realisation. In fact, the will-power of the ignorant who lacks all the technical means to realise his dream forces that intention into form and succeeds. It is that struggle for realisation which is the impressive achievement of the Naïve painter. In a strange way he has pulled it off. The scene in its ghastly nakedness stands revealed, and we are forced to see it too. For a moment we can look with our eyes into his mind; this is how the world appears to him. In other words, this is what the world is to him, because they did paint their own truth.

The important point is the Naïve *vision*, not the lack of skill that makes the Naïve quality. It is not that most of them cannot paint, that is easily forgivable, but that they see the world as they do which is so worrying, and it is that worrying quality which is another reason for their acceptance, because a search for the non-logical, for the un-expected and the absurd, was becoming a concern of the sophisticated painters. Surrealism existed long before the Surrealist movement as such had formulated itself. The Naïve vision allowed a glimpse into the sub-conscious, uncorrected by knowledge, though it was the Naïve painter's consciousness which was unaware of the revelation it produced for others. Like a child, he grapples with objects that meet him; unprepared he has to grasp them in their roundness and solidity, he cannot hold a mental image, it must become a material image. Only absolute certainty and possession reassures him.

What has yet to be analysed is how the genuine Naïve transforms his vision into his picture, in brief, what a stylistic analysis would yield. Mahlow, who was the first to make the attempt to put into a discipline this undisciplined activity, notes on perspective that the two extreme possibilities exist; the Naïve either vastly exaggerates classical perspec-tive, or he abandons it altogether. We thus find ourselves in two different sorts of unreal space. He further notes that nearness of vision of all objects, no matter how near or how far they happen to be, they are all painted alike.[50] Thus we receive an exaggerated clarity, a more than real exactitude, in the attempt to achieve a palpable, graspable reality, yet this escapes willy-nilly into a Surrealist sphere, where everything becomes concrete and dream-like at the same time, where everything has an equal value in the order of things. The view-point of the Naïve is to have none, to be not aware of having to choose. The Naïve painter has always arrived, he never begins to build a new world, he lives in his world, he is happy with what he finds. To call this 'truth' would be naïve, because truth implies exactly choice and selection. To be simply aware is being naïve. The Naïve painter has no doubts, he is totally uncritical. Art, like thought, is traditionally based on system and order. It is an acquired set of rules under which objects and appearances are to be apprehended. With the Naïve painters these rules are not abandoned, because they have never been known. We are thus looking into a pre-intellectual formation and can observe the process of the Naïve painter coming to terms with a baffling, because unsystematised, reality.

It should not be assumed that there is anything like a genuine naïve vision, because that does not exist. All knowledge comes from experience and without experience there is no vision. What is called 'naïve' is 'relatively naïve', but the owner of that relative naïvety is very much the product of his surroundings with all the prejudices, sentiments, emotions and other acquired characteristics of his milieu. The world of the ignorant is primarily unhistorical; the ignorant have no sense of history,[51] a terrible but true statement. In the naïve world picture time stands still. There is no before or after, there is only now. The very idea of history contains the thought of change, but that is too much to expect of the naïve mind. They hold the fundamentalist position, things are as they are; one cannot state it in more primitive form than that, and the term fundamentalist is used deliberately because it contains the firm belief in the revealed truth. If every word is true, there is no argument and no doubt. Religion and primitive thought have their fundamentalist position in common, all else is apologia. The Naïve painter is naïve not only in his means of expression, but also in his mind, his thought and emotions, but it would be quite wrong to consider him unspoilt. He is affected by all the prejudices of the submerged class; he shares a culture with petty tradesmen, village people, small officials. His is the voice that rarely comes to the surface.

It is one thing to accept Naïve art for what it is, but to gloat over it and admire it for its delightful innocence is to fall into the trap of anti-intellectualism and naïvety itself. The sophisticated artists were in no such danger, as their use of primitive forms was deliberate and controlled. Picasso: *Head*, 1908 (Plate 59); Derain: *Head of a Woman*, 1910 (Plate 60) is decidedly Byzantine, though Derain himself was one of the first to discover primitive masks. During the same years the German Expressionists of the Brücke had discovered primitive art in Dresden: Kirchner: *Negro Girl Lying down*, 1910 (Plate 61). These few pictures show the importance of primitive forms for the development of the artists who used them. No such use could have been made by the Naïve painters.

Paris was the centre of the discovery of the Naïve and the key figure is Rousseau, le Douanier. After his discovery others were found in the suburbs of Paris and the process spread further afield until, not unexpectedly, one found many others in outlying peasant communities in Roumania, Yugoslavia, and Hungary. In the United States there is a whole string stretching over two centuries. These were honestly untutored and unskilled painters who knew no better and whose incompetence, reinterpreted as charm, is now being reassessed under the aesthetic of the Naïve. When we come to see the work of Rousseau, we must not be confused by the dates, because Rousseau had been painting a long time before he was discovered. His date of birth as a man is 1844, as a painter, around 1880, and he was only discovered as an artist in 1906, shortly before his death.

Plate 59. Pablo Picasso: Head 1908
     Oil 62·3 × 43·2 cm. *Private Collection*

Liberty inviting the Artists to take part in the 22nd Exhibition of the Salon des Indépendants, 1906 (Plate 62). This genuine populism goes back to the French Revolution which had opened the Salons to all painters, but this had been abandoned until an Independant Salon was created where, incidentally, Rousseau was discovered. The picture has the true qualities of the art of the dispossessed, it reminds one of a mid-nineteenth-century trade-union banner.

The Sleeping Gipsy of 1897 (Plate 63) is a much more genuine Surrealist experience than any of the deliberate works of the later self-conscious Surrealists. It has a poetical intensity which few other pictures can surpass. *The Dream*, 1910 (Plate 64). These paintings exemplify the childish desire to grasp the materiality of objects and hold them down

Plate 60. André Derain: Head of a Woman 1910
Oil on canvas 32·4 × 30·1 cm. *Private Collection*

Plate 61. Ernst Ludwig Kirchner: Negro Girl Lying down 1910
Oil on canvas 64 × 92 cm. *Kunsthalle, Bremen*

Plate 62. Henri Rousseau: La Liberté invitant les Artistes à prendre part à la 22e
Exposition des Indépendants 1906
Oil 175 × 118 cm. *Private Collection*

Plate 63. Henri Rousseau: The Sleeping Gypsy 1897
Oil on canvas 51 × 79 cm. *Museum of Modern Art, New York, gift of Mrs Simon Guggenheim*

Plate 64. Henri Rousseau: The Dream 1910
Oil on canvas 203·2 × 297·2 cm. *Museum of Modern Art, New York, gift of Nelson A. Rockefeller*

firmly, but that is only the means; the genuine poetry of the work and the uncanny control of its inner reality is something which only an artist of considerable quality achieves.

The famous portrait of *Pierre Loti* (Plate 65), originally painted in 1891–92, repainted in 1910. Let us be frank – we think it is funny, but it is not meant to be. The Naïve painter is using a language which he takes seriously. The painter is using a childish language for what is, to him, serious concern. He is in earnest and we cannot take it seriously; to us such a portrait can be written in another language. In fact, we are getting into a semantic, that is a stylistic, muddle. The painter's speech and ours is on the opposite side of knowledge, hence the embarrassment. The same situation arises in the endearing and wholly honest pictures of his own Muse and his friends. As a painting it is very similar to those produced by the American Primitives, for the simple reason that they aimed at academic perfection and had never been supplied with the know-how.

One can distinguish two tendencies among the Naïve painters. For the one tendency, one might adopt the term 'Naïve realists'; for the other 'Naïve Surrealists'. But let us be careful, is it their Surrealism or ours? Is it not more likely that what strikes us as incongruous strikes them as believable? Are we not trespassing not only on the Naïve vision of reality, but also on the Naïve vision of the miraculous? Are we there seeing what religious people really see, and are we there not much nearer to the state of faith than the sophisticated imagery of the official art of the Church? Was not the whole Gothic and Renaissance world of art, the vision of the theologians and humanists, an educated vision? Has not possibly the actual religious imagery of the credulous escaped our knowledge? But an even more terrible thought: could not what we think of as their Surrealism actually be their Realism? Do we know how concrete a vision is formed by the superstitious, how firmly grasped and cherished is their peculiar faith in the unbelievable? Do they, in fact, draw any line between dreams and reality? Does the myth in their eyes take on forms which they accept as tangible? In short, do they think in abstractions at all, or only in reifications which to them become chunks of reality? The illiterate take everything literally.

The Hungarian painter Csontvary (1853–1919) was an almost exact contemporary of Rousseau. He did have some unsatisfactory academic training, but his Naïve vision got the better of his undeveloped skill. *Pilgrimage to the Cedars*, 1903 (Plate 66). What is so marked is the innocent sense of wonder, the light becomes an almost religious illumination. *Mary's Well at Nazareth*, 1908 (Plate 67) may serve as an example of the unwitting Surrealism of a naïve mind.

Another problem is raised by artists coming from a peasant and not a

Plate 65. Henri Rousseau: Portrait of Pierre Loti 1891–92 (repainted 1910)
Oil 41 × 33 cm. *Musée des Beaux-Arts, Zürich*

Plate 66. Tidavar Csontvary: Pilgrimage to the Cedar 1907
Oil on canvas 198·8 × 205·2 cm. *Private Collection, Budapest*

Plate 67. Tidavar Csontvary: Mary's Well at Nazareth 1908
Oil on canvas 380·6 × 550·8 cm. *Private Collection, Budapest*

city surrounding. The line between peasant art and naïve art is a very
thin one and to make the confusion worse, some peasant countries teach
naïve art, as children are told to do children's drawings. Hegedusic,
born in 1901 in Croatia, is the teacher of a whole school of Primitives
and his work strikes one as somewhat faux-naïve. *Innondation* (Plate
68). One of his pupils appears more sincere and more gifted, Generalic,
born in 1914, also Croatian. His peasant pictures are mainly naïve in
treatment, skilful in the use of space and in content as true as a fairy
tale, they look so unsophisticated that they make one think of a higher
sophistication. They could come out of a play by Brecht (another artful
faux-naïve). They remind one of Brueghel, Brecht's favourite painter,
and they are too good to be quite true.

Considering Chagall, one must be very careful to distinguish between
his early work in Russia and his later work in Paris. It is the popular

Plate 68. Krsto Hegedusic: Innondation
Oil on canvas 105 × 132 cm. *Moderna Galerija, Zagreb*

peasant village tradition which lives on in Chagall. From his early pictures from Vitebsk one understands his sources and understands that the acceptance of Chagall by the avant-garde of Berlin and Paris was based on a profound misunderstanding. But this misunderstanding has its root in the readiness to accept any statement that was direct, unspoilt and naïve. It was used as one more nail in the coffin of the academic work of art. In Tsarist Russia the peasants were very fond of a particular sort of icon which was sold at village fairs. The Greek Orthodox Church tried to suppress them, but they always turned up again. They showed the Virgin Mary crudely painted, lying down with legs open, giving birth to a child, or the Virgin Mary with the Christ Child happily glowing inside her womb. This was the way in which peasants understood and visualised the sacred legend, naturally and believably. Chagall *Pregnant Woman* (Plate 69). This is possibly the best surviving illustration to make the icons believable. Here Chagall is wholly naïve. Chagall, however, goes far beyond the naïve; his power of invention goes beyond the dream and the village and will soon and easily merge with the attempts of modern cosmopolitan artists. In all the pictures, even of his earliest years, the Naïve vision finds forms which are far from naïve. *I and the Village*, 1911 (Plate 70) may even be the answer to the question raised, how does Chagall meet his village, how much has he gone beyond it, how near still and how far already is he from the peasant? That is the question he seems to ask himself. In Chagall we encounter the Naïve vision as much as in Rousseau and Csontvary, but in all these a strong poetic quality and occasionally an unorthodox mastery of form makes their work works of art as seen under our perspective.

After Rousseau had been discovered a number of other Naïve painters were taken seriously, all painters of things seen: such as Vivin, born in 1861, and Bombois, who are both genuine Naïves. Nobody can doubt the naïvety of his *Woman seen from behind* of 1928 (Plate 71). Morris Hirshfield, an American born in 1872, is not far removed. See, for example, his *Woman on a Couch* (Plate 72). The concern with funfairs and popular amusements in their miraculous forms are always popular with folk artists. It would be entirely dishonest to say these are good pictures, they are bad pictures, really bad pictures, but what one accepts is the happy sense of the miraculous. Wonders never cease, and for a short moment one sheds all one's own experience and sees the world through their eyes.

Plate 70. Marc Chagall: I and the Village 1911
Oil on canvas 193 × 152·4 cm. *Museum of Modern Art, New York, Mrs
Simon Guggenheim Fund*

Plate 69. Marc Chagall: Pregnant Woman 1913
Oil 193 × 116 cm. *Stedelijk Museum, Amsterdam*

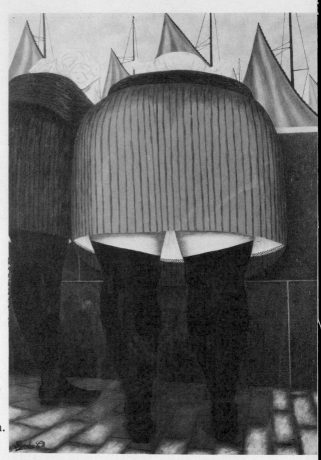

Plate 71. Camille Bombois: Woman
      seen from behind 1928
      Oil on canvas 91·5 × 64·8 cm.
      Collection Ella Winter,
      London

Irreality in Art

There is no unified movement called 'Modern Art'; there are in fact only the paintings of the twentieth century produced by many individual artists, sometimes in isolation, sometimes in groups, some of which even had a programme and issued manifestoes. An investigation of the ideas motivating the artists, which lie beneath the picture, is of some interest within the field of orderly chronological art history. The actual history of modern art is not too complex or too complicated. Two trends can be distinguished which show recurring tendencies in the history of art: the protagonists of order, who aim at formal solutions, and the protagonists of the unordered, of what is often called the soul, or what could be described as the formalist and the fantastic approach. It is thus a mistake to treat 'Modern Art' as one movement which abandons the language of representational art and invents new signs and symbols.

Both tendencies depart from the same point of representation, but move in opposite directions and in the process distort the old image of reality. They have nothing in common but their distance from the past and both look equally strange and distorted if measured by the common measure of tradition, that of Renaissance pseudo-realism. The formalists look for the solution of the pictorial problems in the picture and are consciously creating a new reality, they are in intention the classic painters. The fantastics do not accept any reality but that of their own search and thus become the individualist romantics of our day. Yet in both cases the artists are attempting to create a new language of which the signs have to be read in two different ways, one referentially to reality, the other referentially to the soul. The formalists know that art is a convention; the fantastics believe it to be a truth, a hidden truth, a mysterious truth and therefore so much truer than a reasonable truth. There are two approaches: those of a classical, rational disposition who try to impose order on the world, and those romantic, religious painters who try to find a hidden external order in the world, which is called revelation. The rationalist does not claim to have discovered truth, but the seer does.

I shall not attempt to reconcile the irreconcilable. It is my aim to make that superficially obscure but fundamentally important irreconcilability hidden under the term 'Modern Art' as clear as I can. The rational

111

Plate 72. Morris Hirshfield: Woman on Couch 1941
Oil on canvas 66 × 86·4 cm. *Collection Ella Winter, London*

world picture had its counterpart in the visual arts where, as in life and thought, the painter was attempting to give reason its due by painting reasonable pictures which corresponded closely to reality. This task was by no means an easy one, because the representation of reasonable assumptions never was the stock in trade of the painter. His very history is filled with the more or less convincing presentation of dreams, fears, hopes, aspirations, with mythology, classical, christian or contemporary.

The artist, then, has more often than not been fantastic and it is our error to include in this category the nightmares of Bosch but to leave out of that category the Madonnas of Raphael. They are all equally unreasonable, and have their common root in the same religion. Why a well-ordered fantasy, say an Annunciation by Fra Angelico, strikes us as less fantastic than a disorderly Allegory by Bosch, must lie in us and not in the subject-matter. We have been taught to give the semblance of reason even to unreasonable assumptions, such as the bodily Assumption of the Virgin, and have learned to take the form of order for order itself. I suggest that Bosch was nearer to the Christian imagination and Fra Angelico nearer to Christian deception than we commonly accept.

The fantastic in art has a respectable ancestry nearer to the core of its message than the classical order under which so many dreams have appeared in the guise of reason. The fantastic is the field in which art has been at home ever since its inception, but here too one must be careful and discriminating. Because superficially a painting by Klee looks to the uninstructed eye somewhat similar to a cave painting, the cave painters are credited with Klee-like intentions, as if 40,000 years of history had gone for nothing. Certainly this is wholly wrong because the magic practised by the cave painters had entirely different social and spiritual springs from those of any man today. But what is not so certain is that Klee did not aim at a magical communication which in his search for the origins of art he discovered in the paintings of the 'pensée sauvage'. It is a problem of modern art, or rather a problem of the modern artist, that for the first time in the history of art he is not imbedded in one culture, localised firmly in time and space, but that he is open to all the knowledge and all the influences of the past and the present from all parts of the world. He is thus outside a tradition which sets limits. The artist now lives in a near limitless world of sources. That even in such a situation he can dominate his work is admirable, but it needs a different form of discipline from that formerly given by an unquestioned tradition.

The carriers of tradition are essentially languages, the languages of speech, of pictorial representation, of gestures, of modes of feeling and behaviour. Such languages were always changing and their significations were always understood. The modern painter, when looking for new signs and significations, invents by necessity new languages, and it is a fundamental error to see in these new languages resemblances to any older ones. The signs may be superficially similar; the significations are not. But the complications go further. Are the languages of the modern artist wholly private, or do they have the power to make themselves heard? Can one read the signs, or is there no means of knowing? Both questions can be answered by saying that the distinction between the individual and his society is not as sharp as is often assumed. Though the artist speaks a wholly individual language, we are able to understand him, as we too live in his time. It is at this point that the aesthetic fallacy begins to operate and the language of the critic and the spectator falls into the aesthetic trap. He begins to speak about emotions (his), about sensations (also his), about empathy (his), about aesthetic reconstruction (also his own), and what we are listening to is the aesthetic autobiography of the spectator, which is without interest. What is interesting is the work of Paul Klee and if he had produced no more than forms and colours which lead to aesthetic responses by an unknown number of unknown people, he has wasted his time, because there is more in a picture than that involved in the pleasure principle alone.

If it is right that the artist speaks a language, one must attempt an understanding of the language, not an appreciation. We can appreciate a printed page aesthetically, but it does not make for an understanding of the text. And a picture is a text. Like other texts, it can be clear or obscure. Like poetry, it can be ambiguous. It has secret meanings and open meanings, but it always is more than the letters of the alphabet of which it is composed, as the picture is always more than the signs of colour and shape of which it consists. The difficulty begins when one tries to read a new language with the apparatus of an old language, if one tries to see the signs in an old and not in a new way, and if one expects the old grammar and syntax to be operative. This is not the case, and one has to learn that there are concepts for which our spoken language has no words.

To give one example: we have separate terms for yellow and blue, long and short. The Palau Islanders do not, but they have their own words for long-blue and short-blue, round-yellow and square-yellow. In fact, they do not separate colour from extension and in a way they are right. There is no colour without a shape and vice versa. But our form of thought, highly abstract, recognises the concept 'short' detached from a piece of string or a road, and we can think, or think we can, of the abstract yellow detached from any yellow extension or object. The Palau Islander does not. We have to read the works of Klee in just such a different conceptual frame. He is trying to find expressions for concepts which the language of art has not owned before. He is trying to enlarge our conceptual vocabulary and he does so by relating signs in such a way that they signify another state of relation and awareness. This is not unusual at all. When society develops new events, it needs signs and signals to control these events. Nobody invented modern traffic, maybe nobody wanted it, it happened by multiplication; but once it had happened traffic signs were needed and a new language had to be developed which every motorist is obliged by law to learn, and he has to pass an examination to prove that he has done so. The language of traffic signs is readable because it is based on a convention which is binding on all. The language of art is based on a private convention which is not binding at all, and that is where the artist scores, because he does not want to say what everybody knows already, but he wants to say something which nobody yet knows and he wants to make the unknown known. He speaks a personal language for the communication of a personal experience in his time and the language is determined by the experience which is the act of painting itself. In short, the sign and the meaning become identical; the sign carries its significance. It is at one and the same time, to use the terms of Roland Barthes, the *signifiant* and the *signifié* – the signifying and the signified.

To read Klee one has to explore the world of myth where symbolic languages are spoken, formed and dreamt. We are going with him into the world of the fantastic with the open eyes not of aesthetic consumers, but the philosophic enquirer who even in the world of myth does not abandon his reason though he respects the disguises and riddles in which myth presents a truth outside the world of cause and effect, yet a world where sense still operates as sense or as nonsense, where logic is needed in an alogical context because even fantasy, no matter how weird or absurd, remains in the field of human comprehension, as it stems from the field of human creation. Madness itself is not inhuman and as such remains within comprehensibility. There is no need to impose an order where disorder is apparent, but what is disorder but an order disturbed? The disturbance of order, however, was a very deliberate aim of the writers, poets and artists at the turn of the century.

As early as 1896 one of the seminal works appeared, which was to be important for later *ad hoc* manifestations of modern art – Jarry's *Ubu Roi*. Its influence on the artists in Paris is well attested; there is no evidence as far as Paul Klee is concerned, but it is not the evidence one is looking for, but the unity of the spirit which can be shown. In Jarry's pseudo-comical and pseudo-serious system of thought, which he called 'Pataphysique', he established certain untenable principles which were really intended to show the untenability of all principles. His teaching of this huge joke is kept up in France by the semi-serious Collège de

Pataphysique. The principles of Pataphysique can give us at least one approach to the thinking of Klee. Pataphysique is defined by Jarry as 'The Science of Imaginary Solutions'. What is denied is the claim of all other sciences to propose real solutions. The Pataphysicians claim that they are different only in the respect that they know their solutions to be imaginary, while the rest, that is everybody else, still believes that solutions are real. The College establishes teaching chairs in the Dialectics of Useless Knowledge, Crocodilogy and kindred subjects. Not only the language, but the very solutions of problems are approaching the work of Klee. What else does he offer in his work but the Science of Imaginary Solutions?[52]

If we study Klee's work, not forgetting his almost untranslatable titles, we shall be able to establish several new chairs for crocodilogy and other obscure studies. What Klee places in doubt is the incongruity of subjects; to him congruity consists in any form of similarity, be it in sounds or in signs. There are no separate frames of references for concepts of different orders; the frames of reference disappear and the boundaries of different orders are transgressed. That way lies madness, of course, and magic and poetry. Klee creates a new order in which the sciences are abandoned; yellow becomes a concept which penetrates fishes and flowers and summarises them under the concept yellow. Klee establishes a new order of classification, not dissimilar to the old Chinese classification reported by Michel Foucault after Jorge Luis Borges in his *Les Mots et Les Choses*:[53]

CHINESE DOGS

In an old Chinese encyclopaedia the classification of animals is given thus:

(a) those belonging to the Emperor
(b) stuffed ones
(c) tamed ones
(d) suckling pigs
(e) sirens
(f) fabulous
(g) free-running dogs
(h) those included in the present classification
(i) those getting madly excited
(j) innumerable ones
(k) those drawn with a very fine brush on thin leather
(l) etcetera
(m) those breaking crockery
(n) those who look like flies from the distance

Klee then attempts the destruction of our order of categories and definitions. The irrational accepts the basis of rationality; like a heresy it accepts the system to which it is heretic. Klee is comparable to Lewis Carroll. In *Alice in Wonderland*, logic operates in reverse, even the fantastic obeys the rules of a game of chess and where, as in Klee, credibility gets soft on the edges but the rigid forms keep your doubts in check. Klee also operates with the convention where a chess-board pattern holds the spectator firmly in the picture space, but where all his sense data collected from a different frame of reference get in the way of his new adjustment and where he mentally stumbles over familiar landmarks in a different frame. The game is, of course, endless. The spectator can tread the path outlined; he can follow the pattern of thought and action, or he can refuse to fall into the trap. In every case, he is playing the game according to the rules invented by the artist.

There is in modern art a tendency which has to be described as a deliberate flight from reason, and the Surrealists decidedly aimed at unhinging the mind and destroying reason. Klee had no such aim, nor was he opposed to reason. On the contrary, he wanted to establish new relations within reason, complex connections as opposed to plain causal connections. He wanted to widen the possibilities of understanding, not to destroy them.

One way of reaching the comic, the fantastic and the absurd is to remove the boundaries of the spectator's frame of reference, or let several frames interpenetrate one another, to create that unhinging of facts and objects which the dreamer does without deliberation. The fantastic and the comic live in close proximity; half-way between lives the grotesque. All our recognitions are those of the human possibilities; at no point, no matter how fantastic, can one leave the human imagination, and at no point can one apprehend anything supranatural which, if it did exist at all, would by its very existence fall into the field of the natural. What the artists apprehend are the metamorphoses of imagery, and there is hardly a numerical limit to the game. All one must be aware of is that such metamorphoses are games, not actual awarenesses of actual possibilities.

Poetry enlarges the human consciousness of itself, but of nothing else. The Surrealists intended to shatter the barriers of the consciousness to open the way for the influx of the supra-reality. In fact, a Surrealist painting is essentially a non-artistic product, appearing in the accepted form of a painting. It may create a momentary horror, a thrill or *frisson*, it may even make one think, but it is itself not absurd and neither evokes nor contains the absurd. It tells it in a flat language which turns it into literature or illustration. What is new in the allegory is the iconography which accepts the discontinuity of time and space as experienced in dreams as transferable to the static image. Surrealist imagery is con-trived, often cunning, often revealing, but never very astounding. The method is that of the incongruous. Surrealist painting may have heightened our awareness of the incongruous and made it respectable as an experience. The Naïve picture was much more genuinely Sur-realist, because it was conceived by a mind aiming at the opposite and revealing the unordered reason as an actuality, not as an invention. There is one Surrealist, and not the most typical, who has made a contribution to the expression of the invisible. In the work of Max Ernst a real awe, a newness and an awareness of things unknown is found by a creative mind.

The paradox one has to understand is that the fantastic is almost by definition the uncontrolled, be it the dreams, the nightmare, the halluci-nation, while the work of art is also, by definition, the controlled. One cannot paint monsters in a dream. One has to know what one is doing, and the difficulty is exactly how to transmit one's vision undisturbed and undistorted on to the canvas. Klee sets out to paint, and in the process of painting the myth develops. He is operating with his signs which gain their significance in their mutual signification to point to each other. Together they build the world of meaning that is the picture. They are created by a combination of the hand and the mind, without giving priority to one or the other. They are interdependent and the act is spontaneous, determined by both the calligraphy or script, as well as the thought of the artist. The result is neither premeditated nor unconscious. It is operative at several levels of activity at once. The creative mind and the creative execution are co-operating with the artist as observer and actor as one. The result is as much a surprise to Klee (who said as much) as it is to us. He acts as the medium between a form of reality not yet existing and the canvas waiting to receive it. This new reality assembles itself under the guidance of Klee.

Klee is a very disciplined painter who obeys (according to his own statements) the laws of the picture, he follows the pictorial demands. Never, he says, does he set out to paint an idea or intuition; the idea arrives in the process and presents itself to him when it has taken shape. In fact, this living process of creation is Klee's approach to the secret of life, of living things. Klee is mainly concerned with organic growth, with the life of plants and fishes, of new worlds under water, or in the air, with the mysteries of creation. He creates new species by the laws of artistic mutation. He plays the fantastic role of a god who has to invent the shapes of his creatures if one day they are to live and to praise him. He does not recognise the boundaries of the possible and the impossible. There are no laws or limits to make anything impossible. The freedom of creation is not confined to the sphere of necessity. It is active in the field where none of the laws of an already existing reality need operate. Fantasy is just that part of the human imagination which sets out to fly over the borders of the known and the possible into the realm of the more than possible. It is a search for the limitless and thus contradicts art, that is, itself, because art is bound by the limits of the visible. Thus in a strange way fantasy to be visible becomes material, denies itself as impossible, and becomes art.

Following a process which one need not describe as logical reveals an underlying aim of clarifying, not of confusing an issue. It is true the solutions are imaginary, but they are offered as genuine solutions, namely Klee's own. The first two are concerned with well-known problems, not all hitherto solved: the *Guidable Grandfather*, 1930 (Plate 73); *Family Outing*, 1930 (Plate 74); and the famous *Twittering Machine* of the year 1922 (Plate 75); and later, in 1937, the threatening *Revolution of the Viaducts* (Plate 76).

Klee was more of a Surrealist early in his life. The etching from 1903, *Two men meet, each presuming the other to be of higher rank* (Plate 77), is more out of Kafka, though earlier, and is influenced by the work of Kubin, a strange and genuinely insane artist, then famous in Munich where Klee began his work. *The Holy Carrion*, 1902 (Plate 78). The horrific example of Kubin's work are the real nightmares of an alienated mind. In the work of Klee there is no fantastic imagery, rather a fanciful, witty, occasionally whimsical train of thought, groping for pictorial form.

Miro's genuine desire for the comic, together with a mild Surrealist crossing of borderlines, is all that he has to offer. Possibly the great fantasms are outside our imagination and outside our civilisation, because even artists are sceptics, and the fantastic needs a wild ferocity of belief which we lack. *A Beautiful Bird flying through the Gentle Light of the Moon at Dawn*, 1954 (Plate 79).

With Max Ernst we come nearer to the fantastic, intellectually controlled. *The Elephant of the Celebes* of 1921 (Plate 80) is plain Surrealism. In *La Ville petrifiée* of 1912 (Plate 81) a truly fantastic townscape arises, much nearer to Klee than the Surrealists.

Chirico has said: 'So that a work of art may become truly immortal, it must stand outside the limits of the human experience: the average mind and logic are only harmful.'[54] In magic realism, the objects are separated from their surroundings. Though they are all depicted, each thing is comprehended in its incomprehensibility; things become hard, detached, alienated, removed, as if they were imprisoned in a cage of glass. There is engendered a feeling of dread, the world resembles the dream. With all the trappings of realism, including exaggerated and multiple Renaissance perspective and space, de Chirico succeeds in

Plate 74. Paul Klee: Family Outing 1930
Coloured pen drawing 40 × 57·4 cm. *Klee Foundation, Berne*

Plate 73. Paul Klee: Guidable
Grandfather 1930
Pen and ink 60·2 × 46·2
cm. *Klee Foundation,
Berne*

Plate 75. Paul Klee: Twittering Machine 1922
Watercolour, pen and ink 40·6 × 30·5 cm. *Museum of Modern Art, New York*

Plate 76. Paul Klee: Revolution of the Viaduct 1937
Oil on canvas 65·1 × 48·8 cm. *Hamburger Kunsthalle, Hamburg*

Plate 77. Paul Klee: Two men meet, each presuming the other to be of higher rank
1903
Zinc etching 11 × 19 cm. *Victoria and Albert Museum, London*

conveying the complete standstill of time and space. We are looking into a frozen eternity of reality; all the objects are there, but they are only there, unrelated to anything. It is the fixity of the haunted image of a dream which is real, failing to connect with anything. The suspension of time and space made de Chirico the spiritual and technical forerunner of the Surrealist dream-space. *The Nostalgia of the Infinite*, 1913–14 (Plate 82). There, too, the will of order prevails over the fantastic, or rather, the fantastic itself takes the form of order and geometry. The deliberate creation of an alogical content leads to Surrealism. The aim is not the construction of new space, but the disturbance of the human mind. All logical relations are put in question and new possibilities of non-causal juxtapositions create that possibility of the fantastic arising out of the real.

Dali produces delicately or indelicately manufactured articles of sophisticated consumption. In capitalism even dreams have become commodities, though that is the social condition; the artist, in this case Dali, manufactures them all too successfully. *The Persistence of Memory*, 1931 (Plate 83).

Plate 78. Alfred Kubin: Sacred Carrion 1902
Nymphenburger Verlagshandlung, Munich

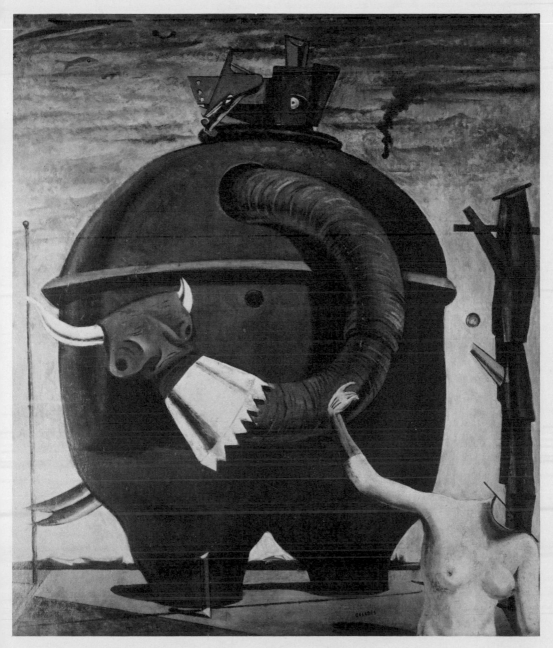

Plate 80. Max Ernst: The Elephant of the Celebes 1921
   Oil on canvas 124 × 107 cm. *Collection Sir Ronald Penrose, London*

Plate 79. Joan Miro: A Beautiful Bird flying through the Gentle Light of the Moon
   at Dawn 1954
   Oil on canvas 30 × 23 cm. *Private Collection*

Plate 81. Max Ernst: La Ville petrifiée 1912
Oil on paper on plywood 30·5 × 58·4 cm. *City Art Gallery, Manchester*

Plate 82. Giorgio de Chirico: The Nostalgia of the Infinite 1913–14
Oil on canvas 134·6 × 63·5 cm. *Museum of Modern Art, New York*

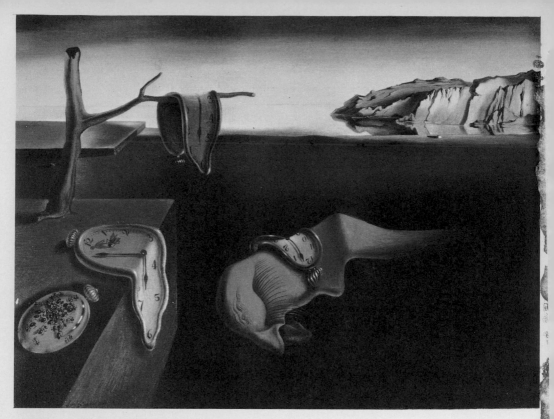

Plate 83. Salvador Dali: The Persistence of Memory 1931
Oil on canvas 24 × 33 cm. *Museum of Modern Art, New York*

The most modest of the Surrealists is possibly the most successful. Magritte knows one important truth: a joke can only arise from the deliberate mix-up of two, and only two, different frames of reference. In Magritte one totally unexpected event occurs in an expected reality, or an expected event occurs in an unexpected reality: *The Red Model*, 1935 (Plate 84). Magritte is successful; he creates the fusion, the surprise, the joke. But one only laughs once; after that recognition expressed by laughter, the picture holds no more secrets. Yet the horrible thought, that our shoes could grow toes, or that our toes could grow shoes, lingers on. Here we enter the field of science-fiction, which is in truth an extension of Surrealism. That some of it may even come true does not diminish but heighten the terror. The borderline between art and life is not fixed but shifting and they are only two different interpretations of a rather bewildering totality.

128

Plate 84. René Magritte: The Red Model 1935
Oil on canvas 73·5 × 49·1 cm. *National Museum, Stockholm*

7

Abstract and Concrete

The very idea of abstract art is the necessary and logical outcome of the concept of the picture existing for its own sake. When the work of art speaks only about its own being, then it has become the sole reason for its existence. It is such a logical conclusion that it had to be expected, but logic has never been enough to understand art. What is needed is a higher form of logic which is called dialectics. Dialectics considers logic to be valid up to the point where its own contradictions result in the negation and then in the negation of the negation, out of which something new arises which is the result and the resolution of the inherent contradictions. The paradox with which we are concerned will be the resolution of how the abstract becomes concrete, or how it becomes nothing. The logic of Malevich leads to the white square on white, or pure invisibility; it has negated the visual arts. The other non-logical but dialectical inversion of abstraction leads to the concretisation of the invisible and thus returns to the world of visibility. That both these roads lead via metaphysics and mysticism is not a necessity of thought, only an accident, perhaps a necessary accident for the artist involved because the jumble of thoughts and theories and the statements made by the artists serve as an attempted rationalisation of their doings. The storehouse of the collected intellectual bric-à-brac of their life is connected with their work.

This study began with the social position of the artist and has followed the different responses which the artist, in conformity with his new situation and his own temperamental endowment, has attempted to make. We could distinguish between the seemingly objective and seemingly subjective attempts at solving his problem, but it is impossible for an artist at work to be wholly objective or wholly subjective. The most objective statement is made by his personality and the most subjective statement has still to be made in the form of an object, the picture itself. The abstract artist attempted to escape from this dilemma, but he had to fail, because no one is able to transcend the boundaries within which he exists. The illusion of that transcendence has various names. The trouble, however, with all mystic transcendentalists is that what they claim to see they believe to be outside themselves; in truth, it is inside themselves. No mystic, therefore, tells us anything about this world or the next, but always something about himself.

The uniqueness of each person is commonplace, because it is that uniqueness which he has in common with everybody else. The question is directly related to the problem of art: the artist, sharing his uniqueness with everybody, is ordinary. What he then has to achieve is transcending his uniqueness by becoming general or universal. It is thus not a paradox, but within the field of expectation when he claims that in his work he is giving us equivalents of universals, and the artists believe they can do it.

It is here that one can find a key to the work of Kandinsky, Mondrian and Malevich. All of them, highly individualist painters, claim in their writings that they do not give us personal statements but universal statements. Hence all are concerned with the idea of the absolute. Their abstractions, then, are not abstractions from sense data or objects but are, on the contrary, absolutions. Absolutions from what? From the prevailing sin of individualism, they are the absolutions of the self. The artists are the seekers after universal, that is, abstract, truth. They have to give us this absolute impossibility in concrete form, so concrete that the form is nothing but itself. It is freed from all associations with reality or recognition, it is not to remind the spectator of anything but itself, it is its own shape, colour, and truth. It is, in fact, a philosophical concept in concrete form. This is an embarrassment, but it is their embarrassment, not ours, and a very old one. It is we who turn the tables on them and see in their work exactly the individual artist's hand-writing and symbolism. We are the ones who analyse their individual style or idiosyncrasy, exactly what they have been at pains to hide or to explain away.

The most logical exponent of this dilemma was Malevich, who was approaching the state of invisibility which cannot any longer be misinterpreted. He was nearer the absolute, which is a polite word for the nothing, than anyone else and he became practically silent in the picture. Kandinsky and Mondrian were still talking in the picture. Malevich was silent, Mondrian was taciturn and terse, Kandinsky loquacious and verbose, and they were all talking about the same thing – about nothing. They expressed it by the thing itself, because that is what abstract pictures consist of, the thing itself, in its ideal form of itself. Some abstract painters saw the ideal as geometrical by necessity, but Kandinsky was at first more liberal and saw that 'form' itself can have any shape, because any shape is a thing in itself. But later he abandoned this complete logic and by trying to be more logical imprisoned his universalist fantasy in the strait-jacket of geometry. It made no difference because geometrical forms are neither more nor less absolute and concrete than any others.

The one thing – and this is truly the dividing line between the abstract Suprematists and all others, even Klee and Miro – is that they were in no way concerned with life, neither with people nor plants nor animals nor objects, or any experienced part of reality; they were concerned with universals, with abstract thought, and in their search for cosmic equivalents they became the writers of their own pictures which bear not the slightest resemblance to the unknown, but are unmistakably the works of the painters, known to themselves and everybody else as Wassily Kandinsky, Kasimir Malevich, and Piet Mondrian. Their true biography as artists is their work, all else is a form of theology.

In abstract painting not only space but even place had to be abandoned. There is not even a hint (as with Braque or Picasso) that a woman was seated on a chair somewhere. In abstract art, no space or place indication is left. There are also other ways of approaching the fact that life disappears completely from the picture. Could it be explained as a gesture of despair that no common experience can be expressed in a work of art, that the isolated individual despairs of his ability to speak to others? Some indications of this can be found in the growing concern to speak to the like-minded, the few friends, to those who understand art – or more often 'my' art.

Or should one approach the question objectively and state that the artists reacted in the only possible way because the subject-matter of the picture had lost all interest and that only its formal qualities had any significance? Were, then, all those artists who devoted their search to pure form freed from subject-content, the painters who carried the new demands to their correct solution, the new creators? Or is their despair a form of nihilism which consciously or unconsciously aims at the destruction of the picture, of art itself? This may not be true for the three painters under discussion, but that nihilistic tendency based on the realisation that art is dead was the motive of Duchamp, who said as much. He 'invented' the *objet trouvé*, the ready-made, by taking an object out of its context and putting it on a pedestal (the pedestal of art) and calling it art. What he did was actually philosophically tenable. By taking the object out of its frame of reference, by placing it in the aesthetic as opposed to the practical functional frame, he did change the object from a lavabo to a piece of sculpture, confirming in the process that the individual piece of art only operates as such in the setting of the artistic reference co-ordinates, or less precisely expressed, the aesthetic expectation.

In the process of the artists' activity, a self-destroying tendency develops which has been a continuing exercise of the destruction of the concept of art as a separate, and in itself different, form of activity. This is, in fact, the more revolutionary position, but instead of giving up painting as art, as Duchamp did, these painters who continued to paint were giving a new apologia to the process. The petty-bourgeois role of 'abstract' art is exactly its replacement of concrete reality, by making the work of art concrete and social life abstract. In short, the problematics of art and the concept of art are raised by the artists themselves as a response to their social position, and more than that, as an answer to the non-existent social role of art. Because, strange as it may sound, the one thing no artist accepts is that his own work is no more than an object of aesthetic sensation giving pleasure. Exactly what the broad public expects of a work of art is what the artist does not recognise as its function. If ever there was a case for the insufficiency of the aesthetic approach, abstract art is the prime example.

The historian may be trying to impose a logical interpretation on the progress of modern art which the process itself did not contain, but even if that is so, he is still justified because the logic of events as they happen, and the logic of the same events as they are seen to have happened, is not the same process. It is wrong to accuse historians of establishing logical connections where none exist. What is wrong is to impute the logic of the historians to the actors and perpetrators of the deeds. What the historian has to see are the limitations and boundaries given by time, thought and social life, and to see how narrow these boundaries are. Within them all is freedom and almost anything possible is possible; without, all is constraint and everything is impossible. This is the field of conflict between the free will of the artist and the determinants of social reality.

The process of artistic creation operates no differently from any other process. What appears as logic is nothing but the outcome of the contradictions within necessity. There are the social limitations which the historian may see and the artist be dimly aware of, but the limitations he sees very clearly are the pictorial limitations. One has to consider the history of art before realising that in the past there were strict limitations, to both form and content. That absence of limitations is in truth the central problem of art today. Goethe has said 'In der Beschränkung zeigt sich erst der Meister'[55] ('Mastery can only show itself within limitations'). It is the overcoming of difficulties which produces the masterly solution, but if there are no social limitations the artist himself has to set them and work within these limits, hence he makes the law and has to fulfil it. This is the formal or stylistic problem of the artist. Having to find his own solution to the problem he has set himself is only another way of saying that the artist had no given task imposed by social needs. He thus becomes a completely self-centred, self-employed, self-expressing person with nothing to do but what he intends and invents. This is the problem of meaning or content of the work. To have no task and no content appears to the artist as an intolerable situation from which he tries to break out. Hence arises the claim voiced by the artists that in fact they do not speak for themselves, but for the whole universe. They cannot claim to speak for any class or group or interest in society. By an inversion of their true isolation, they make the extreme claim that through them speaks the voice of the world.

The meaning of the work of the painters can be elucidated by their own statements. We shall find that in the most orderly, clinically clean pictures by Mondrian and Malevich a truly Messianic madness lies hidden, a form of monomania, an extreme concern with one and only one solution, that search for the one infallible cure of all ills, that panacea which will not only solve all worldly but all spiritual problems, in truth that religious mania which searches for one explanation and therefore one answer to all questions. One of the recurring manifestations is that of purism, a search for utter purity which borders on invisibility, a difficult problem for a visual artist, but one he will attempt to solve by sacrificing all. The search for purity in the picture is an expression of the search for the purity of art, a concept only possible at the moment when art has no purpose but itself.

The terms abstraction, abstract art, non-representational art, non-figurative painting are all of them not satisfactory. The very opposite term, concrete art, or absolute art, is nearer to what the artists themselves intended. The picture itself was to be the concrete reality, owing nothing to association or memory, of another reality being not abstracted but created. The *Oxford English Dictionary* defines 'abstract' as separated from matter, practice or particulars, ideal, abstruse, opposite to concrete; and 'to abstract' as to derive from, to separate in mental conception, to consider apart from the concrete, all of which is not quite what the artists intended. But the *O.E.D.* defines 'absolute' as the abstract, the ideal, and that is much nearer to what they meant. To them, 'abstract' is not a sufficient definition, because all other art, representational, figurative and narrative, is abstracted from something, because every painter gives an abstraction of a reality. Not so the absolute painter, whose reality owes nothing to any other form of reality. Thus his work is not abstracted, but is itself concrete and absolute; that there is a contradiction cannot be denied, but we are faced with an absolute aim and a concrete result.

Franz Marc, the friend of Kandinsky, said that the great problem of the present generation was the rediscovery of the inner mystical construction of the world: 'Perhaps,' he said, 'the European eye has poisoned and distorted the world. – My instinct leads me from the animal towards an abstraction . . . in which the feeling for life sounds

purest to me. – What we expect from "abstract" art . . . is not to make
our agitated soul speak, . . . but make the world itself speak its voice.'[56]
This is really a definite turning away from Expressionism, where the
agitated soul was to speak. The aim now proclaimed is that the world
itself should be allowed to have its say. What he means by the world is
best translated as 'cosmos', or 'the universe'. The aim is the search for
the metaphoric forms which are the equivalents of eternal truths, the
essence; the essence and not the semblance is to be the subject of art.
'Semblance', Marc says, 'is eternally flat, take it away, . . . think your-
selves away, together with your picture of the world – the world will
remain in its true form, and we, the artists, sense this form, a demon
gives us the power to see between the cracks of the world and in dreams
he leads us behind the coloured stage of the universe.'[57] This is a key
sentence for understanding the nature of abstract art. The metaphoric
forms are the forms in painting which are to stand for the equivalent of
the invisible forms of the world. The artist feels that he has these true
forms of the only reality in his grasp, and that this picture is an equivalent of the universe. He thinks of his art as symbolic, and here the nature
of the symbol is important. A symbol is not only a sign, it is the painter's
metaphor (Gleichnis) for a higher truth; these abstract forms are thus
symbols for the essence of being.

In the years around 1910 the problem begins to formulate itself in
the minds of the artists. Kandinsky's book *On the Spiritual in Art*
appeared in 1912. 'Abstract painting', Kandinsky said later, 'does not
exclude the connection with nature, on the contrary, it will become
stronger and more intensive than ever in recent times. . . . Abstract
painting leaves behind the "skin" [that is the outer appearance] of
nature, but not its laws. Allow me to use a big word, its cosmic laws. . . .
An abstract painter receives his "stimuli" not from any old piece of
nature, but from nature as a whole, of its manifold manifestations,
which in him summarize themselves and lead to the work. This syn-
thetic basis finds its most suited form of expression in "non-representational" expression. Abstract painting is broader, freer and fuller of
content than "representational" painting.'[58] Not the question of form
is important, abstract or representational, but its content (spirit, inner
harmony). In abstract painting 'the pure sound comes to the fore, the
soul reaches a state of . . . vibration'.[59] He argues that inner harmony
can be better achieved by avoiding the depiction of the object, because
with representational painting the impact remains with the senses, that
is, with understanding. Therefore 'its beauty does not go towards the
spirit, but away from it'.[60] Kandinsky says: 'Practical sense destroys
abstract sense.'[61] The art of the real must avoid the abstract, abstract
art must avoid the real, and now comes a key sentence: '*By reducing the*

objective part to a minimum, the abstract . . . appears as the most powerful real.'[62] 'When a picture . . . is freed from the need to describe an object (thing) it itself becomes the object (thing), its inner form is not weakened by a subsidiary meaning, and gains its full strength.'[63] 'Who knows', he asks, 'maybe all our "abstract" forms are forms of nature, but not the forms of useful objects.'[64] 'Painting searches for new forms, and very few people know that it was an unconscious search for new content.'[65]

The true meaning of Kandinsky's thought and teaching is 'form is content'. Once form has been freed from the need to depict something not itself, it stands alone in the purity of its own meaning. What that meaning is, one cannot say because speech has no pictorial forms, but each artist's pictorial form is a language. The textbooks for that language are missing; once they existed the forms would cease to hold the meaning they now hold, because they would then hold the textbook meaning and they would rather vanish than do that. Kandinsky has said 'Beauty of colour and form is, in spite of statements of the aesthetic and naturalistic . . . observer not a sufficient aim of art. . . . But the superficial impression of colour . . . arouses a movement of the soul. In a sort of echo, other spheres of the soul sound in harmony. Strongly sensitive people are played like violins who, at every touch of the bow, vibrate in *all* their parts. . . . For, even wholly abstract, even geometrical form, has its inner sound, is a spiritual entity with qualities identical with that form.'[66] This is the important statement and the one which lives on in the claims of the artists of today. 'There is not a form . . . which does not say something.'[67]

In a language the signified is the concept, the signifying is the image: this in more modern terminology is what Kandinsky means by saying that the form and the content are to be one. In other words, Kandinsky tries to abolish the two separate functions of the signified and the signifying and claims that what signifies is at the same time the signified, the sign means itself. This then goes further than the hermetic approach; it goes beyond it because hermetic means enclosed, not open to outsiders unless they have the key or the code, but in the absolute painting of Kandinsky there is no key or code with which to read the sign. The sign is the meaning, the meaning is the sign, and you are face to face if not exactly with the absolute, then at least with an absolutist pretention. In brief, the abstract artist is engaged in a quasi-philosophical investigation of the nature of reality; the perception of the senses is excluded and he attempts to find the figuration of a reality unobserved by the human eye and the human understanding. He claims that the true nature of reality is a secret which the artist can divine.

The critical year is 1910, when possibly Kupka preceded Kandinsky in painting the first abstract picture. At first Kandinsky still abstracts from reality: *Study for Improvisation 2*, 1909 (Plate 85); *Study for Improvisation 8*, 1910 (Plate 86); *Battle*, 1910 (Plate 87); *Painting with White Form*, 1913 (Plate 88).

Plate 85. Wassily Kandinsky: Study for Improvisation 2 1909
Oil on cardboard 48·8 × 70·1 cm. *Städtische Galerie, Munich*

In this seemingly simple field of abstract art, one new, and if you like social, question separates itself out, and though not clearly asked as a question and not clearly answered either, that question is implied. The question is: should there be art at all? Two possible answers to this question exist: first, 'Art should be shared by all'; this presupposes something like 'a quality of art' as a rich treasure. The second answer is: 'Art should be abolished'. The artists responded to this dual question, because implicitly they gave both answers in modern art. The problem is how to preserve art and how to destroy art in the process. The development of the work of art itself shows those very problems in a disguised and formal way. The conflict will be: should Art be saved,

Plate 86. Wassily Kandinsky: Study for Improvisation 8 1910
Oil on cardboard transferred to canvas 96 × 69·5 cm. *Volkart Foundation,
Kunstmuseum, Winterthur*

Plate 87. Wassily Kandinsky: Battle 1910
Oil on canvas 94·5 × 130·1 cm. *Tate Gallery, London*

or should Art become part of life and disappear? The spiritual individualist will want to save art, the materialist constructivist will be prepared
to abandon it. The point to make is not the question of the social
function of the artist, but the reflection or distortion of that problem
within the artist himself and the way in which he tried to solve it in his
work (see first chapter). The actual artistic revolution lay in changing
the function of the work of art; in that sense it was a social process.
The artist plus his work had separated himself from the social sphere
and had entered the private sphere. The dilemma was how to reintegrate
in the social process, or how to preserve the conquest of the private
sphere. It was here that the true conflict had to be resolved. What
separated itself out in 'Art for Art's sake' was the aesthetic element
which had previously been no more than the form of the function and
now, having lost the function, remained an aesthetic form *per se*. This
is the core of the problem of the modern movement in Russia and
elsewhere. What is revolutionary in modern art is not only the solutions
of formal problems, but the whole intention and logic behind them.
The logic lies in the development of the work of art as a function of

139

Plate 88. Wassily Kandinsky: Painting with White Form 1913
Oil on canvas 119·4 × 138 cm. *The Solomon R. Guggenheim Museum, New York*

something without a function and that is called modern art, where the work of art becomes its own function.

The question was formulated most clearly by the Russian Suprematists. 'The painter is a prejudice of the past', Malevich has said.[68] There is a truth in that statement, that it is indeed the intention of the artist to make an absolute nothing appear as a thinkable event. In other words, the vision and the acceptance of the spectator has become part of the aesthetic process and conforms to the artist's intention. Malevich, then, does in the opposite way exactly what Duchamp has done; he proves that the concept of art comes before art, and that the expectation makes the work operate as art. This is true in the sense that if art has no other function then it must become its own function, and it takes two variables to make a function, the artist and the spectator. Before the 1914 war Russian artists had already absorbed the lessons of Cubism, Futurism, Orphism, as well as of Art Nouveau. Many Russians (Burljuk, Larionov, Gontcharova and others) had lived and exhibited in Munich. Marinetti gave lectures in Russia in 1914 and Larionov, the husband of Gontcharova, created Rayonism, a variety of Futurism. There was even a Rayonist Manifesto in 1913; the picture was to be built of shafts of light, based on the theories of Signac and Delaunay.

The words which now appear on the scene are abstract, absolute and concrete. The Suprematists ask for absolute painting, that means the separation of the picture not only from the objective world, but from any expression, even from forms. This need not be read as a form of nihilism, but of an utter logic which leads eventually to negation. Even a rectangle is still a form on the picture plane. The new artists tried to eliminate or denaturalise even this last visible trace of reality, and therefore it is called concrete. ' "We don't speak of painting", Malevich said, when he exhibited his famous work of a black square on a white ground.'[69] 'The painter', Malevich said, 'is a prejudice of the past.' He continues: 'We can only sense space if we leave the earth, when we lose all support. . . . The Suprematist canvas represents white space, not blue space. Blue does not give a real appearance of infinity. Vision encounters . . . its limits [in blue space] and cannot penetrate infinity. The Suprematist white . . . allows the visual rays to continue without limit.'[70] The aim is to reduce painting to absolute zero by denying it any expressive possibilities. 'By Suprematism I mean the supremacy of pure feeling in the pictorial arts . . . the ideas of the conscious mind are worthless. Feeling is a decisive factor.'[71] 'When in 1913, in a desperate attempt to rid art of the ballast of objectivity, I took refuge in the form of the square . . . society sighed . . . "All that we loved has been lost. We are in a desert" . . . But that desert is filled with the spirit of non-objective feeling which penetrates everything. . . . It was no empty square I had exhibited, but the feeling of non-objectivity.'[72] Eventually in 1918–19, he painted the white rectangle on white ground and there was little to be seen any more, but one may argue that this does not matter, because Malevich knew it was there. Art, then, claims to be the supreme reality itself. *Black Rectangle and Blue Triangle*, 1915 (Plate 89); *White on White*, 1918–19 (Plate 90).

The Constructivists drew the opposite conclusion from the end of visibility. They proclaimed: 'Art is dead! – Art is as dangerous as religion as an escapist activity. Let us cease our speculative activity [painting pictures] and take over the healthy bases of art – colour, line, materials and forms into the field of reality, of practical construction.'[73]

' "Art" ', Mondrian says, *'is not the expression of the appearances of reality such as we see it, nor of the life we live, but . . . it is the expression*

Plate 89. Kasimir Malevich: Suprematist Painting: Black Rectangle, Blue Triangle
1915
Oil on canvas 71·1 × 44·4 cm. *Stedelijk Museum, Amsterdam*

Plate 90. Kasimir Malevich: Suprematist Painting: White on White 1918–19
Oil on canvas 78·7 × 78·7 cm. *Museum of Modern Art, New York*

of true reality and true life.'[74] We must distinguish between two sorts of reality, that of an individual nature, and that of a universal nature. We shall then not be surprised to find in the simple primary colours and straight lines and right-angles of Mondrian not a game of checks and balances, but a much more philosophical conception. Piet Mondrian is probably the most determined and most purist of all. He aims at plastic construction which avoids limiting forms, so that it may become the expression of objective reality. He says: 'Limited forms always tell something: limited form is descriptive. As long as this type of form is preferred, individual expression must prevail. In pure plastic composition, the unchanging (the spiritual) is expressed'[75] – through what he calls the 'absolute contrasts' consisting only of horizontals and verticals at right-angles. 'New plasticism', as he calls his art form, uses variable measures and rhythms. This gives the human note and combines in plastic art the individual and the universal. Thus rules the equivalence of both aspects of life. His purism, then, lies in his use of straight lines at right-angles; he only uses primary colours – red, yellow and blue – and what he calls non-colour – black, grey and white. He states: 'In order that art may be really abstract, in other words, that it should not represent relations with the natural aspect of things, the law of the *denaturalization of matter* is of fundamental importance. In painting, the primary colour that is as pure as possible realizes this abstraction of natural colour.'[76] His colours must not create natural harmonies, but they must be placed in such a way that they establish different relations from those of their natural association. Abstract art thus becomes concrete, more concrete than naturalistic art. Man can create a new reality. 'Reality' [everyday reality] he says, 'appears to us as tragic, because it lacks balance, and the world of appearances is confused. It is our subjective view . . . of the world which makes us suffer. Art today is important because it gives us the laws of equilibrium.'[77]

Mondrian searches for the salvation of man in his modern surroundings. *Composition in Yellow and Grey*, 1914 (Plate 91); *Colour Squares in Oval*, 1914–15 (Plate 92). There is only one conclusion to be drawn, as I do not believe in 'absolute truth' in any category of thought and this includes art; I doubt that any artist can find it, but it does not matter as there is no absolute truth. We have to be satisfied with relative truths, and these are expressed by man in many forms.

If we accept that there are many metaphors for reality, we shall have learned much, and if we think of the artists as creators of new metaphors, they have added something to our awareness of the unending possibilities of the universe and of human experience. But this historical and dialectical view is not the answer which a mind in search of absolute truth can accept. His problem is a very old one. It is the tragedy of the vision and

Plate 91. Piet Mondrian: Composition in Yellow and Grey 1914
Oil on canvas 61·5 × 76·5 cm. *Stedelijk Museum, Amsterdam*

the symbol, the tragedy of Moses and Aaron in Schönberg's opera:[78]

> MOSES: Oh, God beyond all thought,
> all defining, complex beyond understanding:
> wilt Thou be interpreted so:
> through Aaron, my mouth, in such images?
> Then so I must have made an image: false,
> as all image must be.
> So I am defeated.
> That was all delusion, then. I
> believed before.
> None can, none may, give Him utterance.
> Oh, Word, Word, Word, that I lack!

Moses refused to be an artist, but Aaron, who had made the Golden Calf, was one.

Plate 92. Piet Mondrian: Colour Squares in Oval 1914–15
Oil on canvas 140 × 101 cm. *Stedelijk Museum, Amsterdam*

8

Contemporary Conclusions

In attempting to illuminate some of the more important concerns of the artists in the twentieth century, I have not proceeded strictly chronologically, nor have I adhered very closely to the labels of the many movements, nor have I done justice to all individual painters of merit. I have tried – and hope succeeded – in doing something else; I have tried to find out if there are some genuine historical reasons which can be thought to have given rise to 'modern art', and attempted to formulate in what way the different pictorial solutions appeared to me to answer in one way or another the general ideas prevailing at the time.

While all historians are quite conscious of the fact that each historic period presents some form of unity in thought and style, no one yet has found a convincing methodology which would bind events in the world of thought, attitudes and morals (which Marx would call super-structure) very firmly to the world of material history, economics and social life. The connections are always apparent if not always trans-parent, but there is never a way in which the two could be firmly bound together by some simple law of cause and effect. In brief, the super-structure 'reflects' the real world not in a mirror, but in something far more clouded and less reflective than a good mirror should be. One may compare it to a distorting mirror with a good many opaque patches.

But I do not wish to paint a picture of a non-existent mirror; all I want to say is that art and all forms of mental constructs, though they owe everything, including their nourishment, to social life, nevertheless have their own laws of distortion, also called imagination, which makes something new and not easily recognisable out of the welter of relations which constitute social reality. Any attempt to equate art with a form of direct reflection is bound to fail, because art is exactly the distorted reflection of something else which, even in its real social form, is not easy to disentangle and difficult enough to isolate. But worse than that, the ideological confusion which shows itself in a work of art or literature where it is, so to say, frozen in time, also operates in the social world. False consciousness and ideologies – academic words for prejudices, hopes, fears, attitudes and moral assumptions in all their forms – act in social life, that is, motivate people in their various actions, and these actions are history. If we reserve the concept of ideology solely to the superstructure of art, morals, religion, law and politics, we must also see that these ideological motivations become active. In its 'frozen form', as I shall call it, ideology has become a finished product and in its open, still 'active form' of social life, acts and reacts and produces new changes and attitudes. In that sense, art is a reflection, but an unclear reflection of an unclear situation.

We must distinguish not only two separate uses of the word 'ideology', but also two separate forms of ideology in art. One use of the word ideology implies a set of ideas and beliefs, openly admitted and propagated as such, this is the everyday use of the word ideology. An art form corresponds to a concept of ideology which in its content and story, openly or just mildly disguised in symbolic form, tells the truth according to the lights of the creed. Every moral, civic or religious picture tells its tale in the most convincing and adequate form. The work of art is didactic, it wants to be understood, and therefore it must be open to full understanding. In these forms, the patron, the artist and the spectator are all in agreement. The one is told what the other one has to tell. The more important form of ideology in art, however, is the one where none of the participants is aware of what he is doing, where, in fact, his work is the outcome of an unspoken, yet totally accepted, set of assumptions.

To give a modern example: an ordinary book for young girls takes for granted all the assumptions of woman's role in society. The book, probably written by a woman, is the total outcome of a male-dominated society, where every assumption is totally accepted and the attitudes and moralities implied, totally unquestioned. The book is read and confirms and strengthens all the assumptions already held by the girl who reads it. It needs a revolutionary attitude to question not the quality of the book, or the style, but every assumption on which it is based. The needlework the girl in the book does, the praise she receives, the nice dresses she gets, the dolls she plays with – everything has to be questioned because it is that doll which is the ideology.

If one carries that sort of enquiry into the field of art and literature, one will suddenly wake up to the fact that its products are totally charged with the invisible ideology which has to be questioned in its entirety. The question is a very simple one, but it has not often been asked. The question is: what does modern art really stand for? What can one deduce from it about the state of our society and its beliefs?

Art has been an instrument of power and direction, but is this still the case? I think it is, yet the artist rarely knows what he is doing. Is then all this 'revolutionary' art, decried for more than fifty years by all the conservatives as modern, ultra-modern, subversive, left wing, radical, destructive – is that modern art really revolutionary in any sense but the pictorial revolution, or has it become willy-nilly, counter-revolution-ary, conservative and confusing itself? The answer cannot be simple or clear cut, but the question is nevertheless worth asking.

The bourgeois establishment accepts freedom as a virtue and demands it for the artist. Any attempt to make the artist conform is considered an infringement of freedom. This theory treats art and artists as ineffective, and their work as socially meaningless. But is that the true position, is not the very claim of meaningless art an ideological disguise for the claim that the bourgeoisie has no ideology?

It has always been the aim of the bourgeoisie to generalise its own assumptions and have them accepted as natural. In the field of art the bourgeoisie has been singularly successful. The bourgeoisie's own con-cept of art as a great, profound, unique, spiritual experience for the spectator, and an act of individual creation of the artist as genius, has been accepted almost without doubt or contradiction.

The illusion of creation out of nothing pleases the capitalist entre-preneur, and the concept of the uniquely endowed individual creator corresponds to his own claims and serves as a happy and hallowed model for his own masterful personality; it symbolises and justifies private enterprise and the mystery of profit.

If we regard each work as a fable embodying the myth of the age and the artist, these imaginings and images hold the personal quality of the artist within the collective myth of the group or society. Each work of art thus still contains to this day its fable or content expressed in a multi-tude of personal disguises, and readable not as truth or information, but as myth. The question then arises: is art important or meaningful? Was it a total error of mankind ever to give forms to ideas which, though the form does not, because no form can, correspond to an idea, nevertheless acts as a directing signpost towards the idea which society wanted to symbolise? If such symbolisations are of a social, moral, civic nature, their political and spiritual importance can still be understood. In that sense, the head of the Queen on the coins is a valid work of art. But decidedly all modern works of art are not of that nature, and if they act as symbols of something else, what could be their significance? This is the question to answer. With the rise of individual self-awareness the idiosyncrasies of the individual were considered to be relevant. Society approves and encourages the expression of the totally unique and wholly private idiosyncrasy of each.

We then find a logic in modern art, where Klee is exactly like Klee, because only he is Klee and his every stroke of the pen speaks only of himself; all we can do is to make the acquaintance of that unique character. From this point of view, the work becomes a unique indi-vidual creation unlike any other and as interesting in that capacity as a person whose personal character you may be interested in exploring. Thus we must conclude that the artist does not make a valid statement about anything but his own way of being. This is the logical conclusion.

A much more readable painter like Picasso also makes not a statement about women, but about his own state face to face with that woman. What he paints is his state and not that woman, though to us the picture appears as that woman as stated by Picasso. In other words, he paints because he wants to find out who he is; he paints because he is curious to know what comes next. His whole work is his whole life, as a form of self-exploration and self-definition.

This points towards something like a valid truth in art. Art has always· been a process of the self-definition of society. Art gave those forms and symbols in which society recognised itself. The visual arts are, however, not the only suppliers of symbols of self-recognition; manners, attitudes, laws, ethics, behaviour, are all equally ritualised and binding upon society, and are equal forms of self-recognition. The difference with modern art is not the function of the work of art, which is unchanged, but that it is displaced from the social sphere to the private sphere. It functions as before, but in the intimate sphere and not any more in the public sphere. That change is totally logical as part of the social process in which life has been separated into two parts – the social and the private sphere. The process of work goes on in the practical world from which the individual separates his identity in order to remain an individual. He thus lives in the illusion of his unique individuality which he can only recognise outside his social activity.

There is still a social question and that is why and how was this private art accepted, if not by the public at large, then by groups of understanding admirers, to whom it has become part of their life. The modern work of art is an organisation which contains and expresses a personal experience which others of a similar disposition may be able to share, but this is only possible in a society where personal experience is considered to be valuable enough to be formed, stated and consumed. Art has reached the stage of commodity production. The original remains a status symbol. But this is not the only question, there is also the question of the reproduction, where private art reaches the many, and here the surprise is greater, namely, that there are thousands who identify with Klee.

I do not wish the argument to become circular; because a work of art is accepted, it thereby proves to have been a work of art in the first place. This, however, is the way historians argue when they say that what has not happened is not history. This near circular argument, however, is not new. We accept what we find in a Renaissance palace as art and make only qualitative judgments of good and bad. If in the Renaissance the work served as one element in the self-definition of the man who commissioned it and that is why he actually commissioned it, then the possession of a work by Klee serves the same purpose. It does so, however, at a more idiosyncratic level, because the individual's self-identification is no more with his family, the State or the Church, but with himself. Thus the acceptance or recognition of the modern work of art once more does not become an aesthetic but a political decision, and it is made exactly on these grounds. Though the question of individual taste obscures the problem, the choice itself is an ideological one. Modern self-expression and self-identification is thus seen as part of the bourgeois situation and the one trap to be avoided is to equate bourgeois culture with culture, bourgeois values with values. The bourgeoisie has always attempted to make its own ideology appear as eternal. The attempt to use modern art as one of its props is totally traditional, but this should not prevent us from understanding what it portends, or free us from treating the artist as dependent and the work of art as a piece of ideology.

To deprive the bourgeoisie, not necessarily of its art but of its concept of art, is the precondition of a revolutionary argument.

References

Many of the statements by artists are quoted from a collection of artist's statements: W. Hess: *Dokumente zum Verständnis der modernen Malerei*, Rowohlt, Reinbeck/Hamburg, June 1956.

On Cubism, most relevant statements were collected by Edward F. Fry in *Cubism*, Thames & Hudson, London, 1966.

Where quotations are taken from these collections, the reference is given as: 'W. Hess' and 'Edward F. Fry'. The original source is given as well.

All translations, unless otherwise stated, are by the author.

Introduction

1. '. . . a proposition is a picture of reality'. In *Tractatus Logico-Philosophicus*, Routledge & Kegan Paul, London, 1961, proposition 4·01, p. 37. Translation: D. F. Pears and B. F. McGuiness.
2. *Paragone, a comparison of the Arts by Leonardo da Vinci*, ed. Irma Richter, Oxford University Press, London, 1949, p. 31.

1

3. *Gothic Architecture*, London, 1962, p. 240.
4. 'A Comparison between Primitive and Modern', Exhibition arranged by the Institute of Contemporary Arts, 20 December 1948–29 January 1949, Institute of Contemporary Arts, London, 1949, pp. 6–7.
5. cf. André Malraux, *Le Musée Imaginaire*, Gallimard, Paris, 1965.
6. In Ch. Morice, *P. Gauguin*, Paris, 1919. W. Hess, p. 29.
7. P. Gauguin: *Briefe*, Bâle, 1932. W. Hess, p. 30.
8. Karl Marx: Preface to the *Critique of Political Economy*, London, January 1859. Karl Marx and Frederick Engels, *Selected Works*, in 2 vols., vol. I, Moscow 1962, 5th Impression, p. 363. – 'It is . . . their [men's] social being that determines their consciousness.'

2

9. From 'The Son as the father of the man', *Times Literary Supplement*, no. 3630, 24 September 1971, p. 1134.
10. Hélène Parmelin *Picasso – The Artist and his Model and Other Recent Works*, Harry N. Abrams, New York, 1965, p. 58.
11. Albert Einstein: *Relativity – the Special and the General Theory*, Methuen, University Paperbacks, no. 10, London, 1960, p. 13.
12. *Ibid.*, p. 14.

13. 'Qu'est-ce-que . . . le "Cubisme"?', *Comoedia Illustré*, Paris, 20 December 1913. Edward F. Fry, p. 129.

14. *Ibid.*, pp. 129–30.

15. *Ibid.*, p. 130.

16. Figuère, Paris, 1913.

17. *Méditations Esthétiques: Les Peintres Cubistes*, ed. L. C. Breuning and J.-Cl. Chevalier, Collection: 'Miroir d'Art', Hermann, Paris, 1965, p. 48.

18. *Ibid.*, pp. 51–2.

19. Introduction to the catalogue of the 45th exhibition of the Manés Society, Prague, February–March, 1914. Edward F. Fry, p. 134.

20. *La Morale des Lignes*, Paris, 1908. Edward F. Fry, p. 45.

21. Introduction to catalogue of Braque Exhibition, Galérie Kahnweiler, Paris, November 1908. Edward F. Fry, p. 49.

22. Oto Bihalji-Merin: *Ende der Kunst im Zeitalter der Wissenschaft?*, W. Kohlhammer, Stuttgart, 1969, pp. 49–50.

23. In *Ibid.*, p. 50.

24. Oto Bihalji-Merin, *op. cit.*, p. 50.

25. In *Ibid.*, p. 50.

26. *Méditations Esthétiques: Les Peintres Cubistes*, Paris, 1965, pp. 56–7.

27. W. Hess, p. 50.

28. Paris, 1965, p. 56.

29. *Op. cit.*, p. 56.

3

30. Hélène Parmelin, *op. cit.*, p. 106.

31. *Ibid.*, p. 170.

32. *Ibid.*, p. 49.

33. 'Statement to Marius de Zayas', published as: 'Picasso Speaks', *The Arts*, New York, May 1923, pp. 315–26. Edward F. Fry, p. 166. – 'We all know that Art is not truth. Art is a lie that makes us realize the truth, at least the truth that is given us to understand.'

34. Hélène Parmelin, *op. cit.*, p. 110.

35. *Ibid.*, p. 66.

36. *Ibid.*, p. 10.

37. *Ibid.*, p. 90.

38. *Ibid.*, p. 90.

39. *Ibid.*, p. 10.

4

40. cf. Karl Löwith: *Von Hegel zu Nietzsche*, W. Kohlhammer, Stuttgart, 1964, 5th ed., p. 129.

41. cf. *Ibid.*, pp. 125–6.

42. cf. *The Sources of Modern Art*, Thames & Hudson, London, 1962.

43. Review of G.Fr. Daumer: 'Die Religion des neuen Weltalters', *Neue Rheinische*

Zeitung, no. 2, February 1850. In Alfred Schmidt: The Concept of Nature in Marx, NLB, London, 1971, p. 132.

5

44. Georg Schmidt: 'Was ist ein peintre naïf?'. Essay in catalogue of exhibition: 'Das naïve Bild in der Welt', Baden-Baden, 2 July–4 September 1961, p. 13.
45. Alfred Schmidt, op. cit., p. 153.
46. Collected Works, 4th ed., Vol. 5, Moscow, 1961, p. 111.
47. cf. L. D. Ettlinger: 'German Expressionism and Primitive Art', Burlington Magazine, vol. CX, no. 781, April 1968, pp. 191–201.
48. Op. cit., p. 240.
49. Taken from a secondary, now untraceable, source.
50. cf. Dietrich Mahlow: 'Das naïve Bild in der Welt – Text zur Austellung und zum Begriff Naïve Kunst'. Essay in catalogue of exhibition: 'Das naïve Bild in der Welt', Baden-Baden, 2 July–4 September 1961, pp. 195–6.
51. cf. Richard Hoggart: The Uses of Literacy, Chatto & Windus, London, 1957, p. 158.

6

52. For the above passage, cf. Simon Watson Taylor: 'The Magnificent Pataphysical Posture', Times Literary Supplement, no. 3475, October 1968.
53. Gallimard, Paris, 1961, p. 7. English Translation: The Order of Things, Pantheon Books, New York, and Tavistock, London, 1970
54. In a letter, 1914. W. Hess, p. 111.

7

55. From sonnet: 'Natur und Kunst . . .', Sophien Edition, Weimar, 1891, p. 129.
56. Briefe, Aufzeichnungen und Aphorismen, Berlin, 1920. W. Hess, p. 79.
57. Ibid., pp. 79–80.
58. Aufsätze von 1923–1943, ed. Max Bill, Stuttgart, 1955. W. Hess, p. 87.
59. Ueber das Geistige in der Kunst, Munich, 1912. W. Hess, p. 87.
60. 'Ueber die Formfrage'. Essay in Der Blaue Reiter, Munich, 1912. W. Hess, p. 88.
61. Ueber das Geistige in der Kunst, Munich, 1912. W. Hess, p. 88.
62. 'Ueber die Formfrage'. Essay in Der Blaue Reiter, Munich, 1912. W. Hess, p. 88.
63. Ibid., p. 88.
64. Aufsätze von 1923–1943, ed. Max Bill, Stuttgart, 1955. W. Hess, p. 88.
65. Ibid., p. 94.
66. Ueber das Geistige in der Kunst, Munich, 1912. W. Hess, p. 89.
67. Ibid., p. 89.
68. 'Suprematismus, aus den Schriften 1914–1920.' W. Hess, p. 98.
69. W. Hess, p. 96.
70. 'Suprematismus, aus den Schriften 1914–1920.' W. Hess, pp. 98–9.
71. Kasimir Malevich: The Non-Objective World, Theobaldi, Chicago, 1959, p. 67. English translation of Die gegenstandslose Welt, Bauhausbücher no. 11, Munich, 1927.

72. *Ibid.*, p. 68.

73. Alexei Gan: *Constructivism,* Tver, 1922. In Camilla Gray: *The Russian Experiment in Art 1863–1922,* World of Art Library, Thames & Hudson, London, 1971, p. 256.

74. *Plastic Art and Pure Plastic Art,* Faber & Faber, London, 1937. In Herschel B. Chipp: *Theories of Modern Art,* University of California Press, Berkeley, Los Angeles and London, 1971, p. 359.

75. *Neue Gestaltung,* Bauhausbücher no. 5, Munich, 1925, W. Hess, p. 101.

76. *Plastic Art and Pure Plastic Art.* In Herschel B. Chipp, p. 356.

77. *Plastic Art and Pure Art* (Essays 1937–43), New York, 1947. W. Hess, p. 103.

78. English version: David Rudkin, Friends of Covent Garden, London, 1966, p. 35.

Illustrations

Acknowledgements

Thanks are due to Miss Dorothy Scruton; who not only typed the M.S., improving it in the process, but who also assisted greatly in the selection and location of illustrations.

Thanks are due to the owners, both private and public, for permission to reproduce the pictures illustrated in this book. Details are given in the captions.

For copyright permission we wish to thank S.P.A.D.E.M., Paris (Plates 9, 16, 17, 18, 19, 20, 23, 24, 25, 26, 27, 28, 29, 32, 33, 34, 35, 36, 37, 38, 39, 40, 41, 42, 43, 49, 50, 51, 55, 58, 59, 71, 73, 74, 75, 76, 77, 80, 81), and A.D.A.G.P., Paris (Plates 21, 60, 69, 70, 79, 83, 84).

In many cases copyright photographs were supplied by the owners of the pictures. Additionally we would like to thank the following: A.C.L., Brussels (Plate 12), Service du Documentation de la Réunion des Musées Nationaux (Plates 13, 14, 22, 29, 32, 51), Royal Academy of Arts, London (Plate 54), Landesbildstelle Rheinland (Plate 56), Rheinisches Bildarchiv (Plate 57), Tosodabac, Zagreb (Plate 68).

INDEX